The Pursuit of INTEGRITY

Book 1

Frank B. Calhoun, MD, DMin

An Imprint of
GlobalEdAdvancePress

The Pursuit of INTEGRITY
Copyright © 2016 by Frank B. Calhoun
ISBN 978-1-935434-78-8

Library of Congress Control Number: 2014931841
Calhoun, Frank B., 1947
The Pursuit of LIFE

Subject Codes and Description: 1: REL 006410 Religion: Bible Study – Language Study; 2: REL 006400: Religion: Bible Study - Exegeses and Hermeneutics; 3: REL 006700 Religion: Bible Study- Bible Study Guide

All rights reserved, including the right to reproduce this book or any part thereof in any form, except for inclusion of brief quotations in a review, without the written permission of the author and publisher.

Cover Design by Global Graphics
Printed in the USA

The Press does not have ownership of the contents of a book; this is the author's work and the author owns the copyright. All theory, concepts, constructs, and perspectives are those of the author and not necessarily the Press. They are presented for open and free discussion of the issues involved. All comments and feedback should be directed to the Email: *[comments4author@aol.com]* and the comments will be forwarded to the author for response.

Published by
Post-Gutenberg Books™
An Imprint of GlobalEdAdvancePress
www.gea-books.com

TABLE of CONTENTS

The Pursuit of Integrity 1

Real Integrity 23

Test or Contest 37

Self-Esteem 47

Emotion 55

Sympathy 67

Denial, Defense, and Deception 73

A Name Gone Vain 107

Glossary 115

ABOUT THE AUTHOR

Frank B. Calhoun, MD, DMin, is a Tennessee physician, specializing in Emergency and General Practice. Dr. Calhoun is known for diagnostic skills and the ability to manage multi-system diseases. Through Grace Clinic, he offers comprehensive treatment for patients of all ages, typically providing primary care services. The Pursuit of Life consists of essays written to meet the spiritual needs of his patients. The material was designed as syllabi for Bible study groups.

Dr. Calhoun became a believer in Jesus Christ at the age of 19, while in the U. S. Navy. After graduating from The Medical School of Georgia and Luther Rice Seminary, he and his family went to Indonesia as Medical Missionaries. On his return to the U. S., Dr. Calhoun specialized in emergency medicine. In 1999, God guided him to renew his ministry to others in medicine, but especially in writing and face to face encounters. The product of this work in his life is in your hands – this book. His prayer is that this book will help advance you in "The Pursuit of Life."

INTRODUCTION

The chapters of this book are essays written by Frank B. Calhoun. These works are a component of Dr. Calhoun's Medical ministry at Grace Clinic, where he practices traditional Medicine, and ministers to the spiritual needs of his patients. Grace Clinic is a medical ministry that is biblical, Christian, non-denominational, and which operates with emphasis on God's grace.

The contents of these chapters are the result of learning with the assistance and mentoring of many other teachers of God's Word, formal training through Luther Rice Seminary, and with guidance from the Spirit of Truth (John 14:16-17).

The Reader may contact Dr. Calhoun and Grace Clinic for assistance, comment, or feedback using the address below:

Frank B. Calhoun, M.D., D.Min.
Grace Clinic
II Northgate Park, Suite 104
2158 Northgate Park Lane
Chattanooga, TN 37416
423 802 5222 or Fax 423 531 3495
Email: graceclinicfbc@aol.com

The following four books are available in one volume:
The Pursuit of LIFE

Book 1 --The Pursuit of INTEGRITY
Book 2 – The Pursuit of LIFE
Book 3 – The Pursuit of FAITH
Book 4 – The Pursuit of TRUTH

*"But seek (pursue) first His kingdom
and His righteousness (integrity),
and all these things will be added to you."*
Matthew 6:33

The Pursuit of INTEGRITY

Regardless of where you are in your life, up or down, young or old, educated or uneducated, your quality of life can benefit greatly from the information I am about to provide you. Perhaps you already know all about this. It took a long time to put together all this information and even longer to realize the value of it and apply it to my own life.

Every life, yours included, should have the best possible quality and value. Your Creator wants this for you. He designed you to live a certain way; a way that will serve His purpose for you. At the same time, He will give you stability and even joy regardless of your circumstances; whether you are a genius, a pauper, a jock or a victim! It is true that He did not create everyone equal; obviously people are very different. But, He did provide a way of thinking and behaving that provides happiness for everyone. This is a reflection of His love and justice. He provides for His creatures and because He is fair, He provides what is most valuable for all of them. Everyone can have this internal value which will give you the "success" you need to enjoy your life in spite of your own bad choices, and regardless of the effects on you from the bad choices of others and even the pain and suffering that can come to you from disease, disability or death. The life God designed for you will provide you stability and contentment, even in the face of loss, the threat of loss, and in the face of all kinds of uncontrollable, negative, threatening circumstances.

There is no secular term to describe this character behavior that I am writing about. The reason for this is that the unbelieving secular world does not know it, seek it or need it.

Their needs are external, visible and temporary. Weakness is so epidemic it does not know the name of the solution to its own problem. What I mean is that most of you are satisfied to remain where you are—a position of weakness—therefore you do not seek what pleases your Creator.

He is pleased with the character behavior He Himself is full of. You will have to go to His own Book of Vocabulary to find these words. He is righteousness, justice, truth and love. These are the moral characteristics of God. One word in His word that sums them up is "godliness". Now what word from your familiar vocabulary can you use to represent godliness, to represent the character behavior that will make a noble, stable, successful, wise and highly esteemed person out of you?

Let me clarify that I want to pick a word or term that best describes all that God created you to be . . . a creation that is like Him and therefore pleases Him and so produces a quality of life that is also very pleasing to you. I have considered the word "genuine" because this word is respected by all and everyone likes a genuine person. But think how close to this many other words would be, e.g., zealous, loyal, committed, courageous and sincere. These are adjectives that cannot be absolutely reliable. For example, a person can be a genuine fool, a dedicated and loyal Nazi, and a courageous terrorist. There is good sincerity, and there is bad sincerity (see *Good and Bad Principle*).

The very best word is integrity. There is such a thing as bad integrity, but I will touch on it at a later time. For the purpose of good communication, when I use the term "integrity" I am always referring to good integrity, unless I write otherwise.

God's integrity, alluded to earlier, consists of His righteousness, justice, truth and love. These four characteristics of His include His grace, fairness and mercy toward you—His creature. He is very pleased with His own integrity. He loves His integrity and is impressed with His integrity. When He finds

The Pursuit of Integrity

this integrity in you, He feels the same toward you as He does toward Himself. For additional synonyms, terms, words and metaphors in God's Word for integrity see the addendum. Note that God the Holy Spirit, the author of Scripture, has used many different descriptions of the character qualities that please God. I have taken all these into study and chosen the word integrity to include and express all of them.

And so the person of integrity seeks to please God, therefore, you should become quite familiar with all these words in the addendum. They please God. "To please God" is an idiom itself of what it means to have integrity. A very important method of doing this, one worth memorizing is this:

Love what God loves. Value what God values. And conversely: Hate what God hates. Reject what God rejects.

As a person of integrity, you are a truth seeker. You do not just survive and live for what you can see, hear, taste or touch. You are engaging life's questions about why you are here, how did you get here, and where did "here" come from? Is there a future and how do you get there? Integrity has no apathy. You are not content to be in the dark. You need to be more and more aware of everything, especially yourself, creation and the Creator. Therefore, everything you encounter, that you see, experience, hear or think you know, you analyze it, examine it and strain it through the filter of God's absolute truth. Why?

1. To prevent deception.

2. To learn more (see *Divine Viewpoint*).

3. To clear out garbage (see *Orientation to Life*).

You may have already asked, "What is the connection between integrity's love for the truth and love for God?" Jesus answers this way, "WHOEVER is on the side of (loves) the truth (NIV) listens to Me (God)" (Jn. 18:37). So you see, no one can say he loves truth and at the same time reject the truth (Jesus Christ; Jn. 14:6, "I am the truth . . ."). This is neither logical nor possible. God created truth. To love Him is to love truth and hate error—which He also does. This is why integrity always loves God; because He is the origin and image of integrity. This is logical, and honesty always accepts that which is logical.

Integrity includes honesty, but is much more, as you will see or have seen hopefully already. You can be honest at work, but not at home and vice-versa. You can be honest to a fault and yet be self-serving. You can be as honest as Abe, but still hold on to religion or traditions that you know are ridiculous. I am using "honest" out of a long list of things that are moral because once I set forth the word integrity, the immediate response of many is to think they are honest, and therefore they have integrity. Indeed this may square with the current secular use of the word integrity, but I am using it in a Biblical sense, so remember to include ALL the qualities and behaviors that God loves; those qualities which once gained will insulate and protect you. (All listed in the Addendum).

THE INTEGRITY ANALYSIS

Out of the womb you come with no integrity! You were charming, entertaining, cuddly and you gave a lot of joy to many people. But in spite of such a positive and innocent state of being, you were yet to have integrity. If you had integrity as a child you would never have said, "You can't make me," or, "I will if I want to." Now children are precious, which means that even precious people can be without integrity. I hope you understand my point.

Nevertheless, you are born with four functions, which if used correctly, will get you the integrity you need. (I use this word often. Don't lose sight of it's meaning. Review the addendum.) These four functions are:

The Pursuit of Integrity 11

1. Love or affection. You have a natural tendency to give your affection out to objects or others. You can choose which are the objects of your love.

2. Intelligence or perception. You can learn, understand, and "figure out" things; if you will. This is the area of function where you use your logic. Everyone has the capacity to be logical. For example, if two statements or opinions contradict each other, then everyone knows both cannot be right. This is an example of logic! You can choose to use it to gain understanding.

3. Faith. Everyone has faith, but not everyone puts their faith in the same object. Some trust God, some trust money. You cannot trust both. This is a limitation on faith. You can choose the object of your faith.

4. Volition, choice or free-will. Notice that at the end of the first three functions I told you that you could choose. This is volition. Volition is therefore fundamental or foundational to the use of all your God-given and God-preserved functions. You can use your volition for good or bad. You can choose to self-destruct or advance to integrity.

This fourth function deserves more attention. Understanding its function is vital to achieving integrity. Integrity is a gentlemen just as God is. He gave you a free-will called volition. He lets you use it for good or bad, smart or dumb. We sometimes call this "live and let live", that is, you do NOT force your will on another. This is part and parcel of "loving your neighbor". God expects this from you because it is being like Him. Remember the second commandment. The application of live and let live, respecting the volition of another, prevents a lot of conflict and a lot of stress and at the same time demonstrates integrity. Integrity is always more pleasing and less stressful. In fact, it is stress free!

Another word about the four functions you have. Note the first letter of each one put together in this order spells LIFV, also pronounced Life! This is a memory tool. Use it. You can use or abuse these four functions. If you persist in choosing to not use your "I", or put your "L" and "F" in the wrong places, then you create stress, loss, conflict and a lot of misery. This can happen to the extent that in a time of pressure you are unable to function. You can lose the normal function of your LIFV through a thorough-going abuse of it!

On the other hand, use it wisely with the integrity you have and you will see your integrity compound. The functions of LIFV themselves will become more real, more keen and more effective. Use your LIFV to build your integrity; a status and a life which you cannot lose!

Good love, good intellect, good faith and good volition are all "seeds" of integrity. You plant those seeds and the cycle begins. Bad love, bad intellect, bad faith and bad volition are your worst nightmares; your enemy. Bad love is loving for pleasure or comfort. Bad intellect is arrogance. Bad faith is fear and anxiety. Bad volition is rebellion against what you know to be right. It is rejection of what is true.

Here is an example of the right use of your LIFV:

"I know, my God, that You test the heart and are pleased with integrity" (I Chron. 29:17, NIV).

First of all, notice positive love for God, a good object for your love. Second, note positive intellect, "he knows", something about God and he accepts it. Third, notice he has positive faith in God. He knows what God loves and what He is pleased with. This all is a result of positive volition toward God revealed by the personal "my God".

The Pursuit of Integrity

When God examines your heart, which He does, He is looking at your motives. Motive means why you do what you do. Integrity always has right motive. Bad motive is doing something for self-serving reasons, or doing for no good reason. I Corinthians 13:1-8 is the outstanding passage on motive. It clarifies God's complete concern with good motive. Read the passage. Realize that if you are self-sacrificing and serving your fellow man to the point of death, if you do not have the motive of love, then it is all useless and loss. It was bad work, bad sacrifice and bad service. Faith and hope (confidence) are certainly included in integrity, but if you have both faith and hope but do not have love then you do not have integrity. In fact, in the words of Scripture, "you are nothing!" (v2) This principle is extreme and it is not of this world; not human. In fact, human effort alone cannot produce this kind of life.

The point is that individual, admirable, human characteristics, however celebrated, are not enough. Please understand this point. So I will elaborate: Intensity in faith, service, commitment, morality, zeal, loyalty and courage without love is possible and is tragic because it is LOSS! Remember that love is one of the four components of God's integrity. Could this be why it is such an absolute necessity?

Notice, also, while you are in I Cor. 13:1-3, the LIFV there. It is all there except good love! Point being . . . LIFV works in your behalf and pleases God only when all four components are present and positive. There has to be harmony! It is possible for one of them to rebel, and so hinder the success of all the others.

THE DEMAND FOR INTEGRITY

Integrity is a comprehensive word. It includes morality, ethics and honesty, but it is more than anyone of them. A person can be all of these and still not be a person of integrity! Because, integrity represents the life/mind that actively pursues ALL truth with the right method, motive, humility, and honesty. And at the same time, actively rejects and cleans itself of ALL error, deception and distraction; with confidence and courage, NO fear of change, opposition, criticism or ostracism because integrity chooses truth over people who oppose the truth. This means people who are apathetic to it, arrogant about it or offended by it. A person of integrity is unstoppable in his love for truth, seeking truth, learning truth, obeying truth and expressing truth. Integrity cannot tolerate partial truth, double truth, hiding truth or outlawing truth.

In addition, integrity is actively pursuing the very best value system; right values that lead to right priorities that lead to right goals. Because of the humility factor included, there is complete submission to authority; the Creator. Submission is critical. It is the core of humility, without which you cannot be taught, you cannot love properly and you cannot serve. This is why Jesus said in John 7:18, ". . . but He who works for the One who sent Him (submission) is a man of truth (integrity), there is nothing false about Him." This is another statement by Christ that real integrity is only found in a right relationship with God. Without humility there is no integrity. Why is this true? Because self-serving lends itself to dishonesty and pride. Anyone who rejects the authority of their Creator puts themselves in the position of weakness. Once you serve yourself, you value what you think over what God thinks. When you overvalue what people (including yourself) think, then you will concern yourself with their opinion of you; truly a weak position. Integrity is not weak. Note what one of Jesus' enemies said about Him in Matt. 22: 15-16 (NIV), "Teacher, we know You are a man of integrity and that You teach the way of God in accordance with the truth. You are not swayed by men, because You pay NO attention to who they are."

Note carefully here that it is not arrogance that pays no attention to who people are, but it is integrity, which includes humility. To be "swayed by men" means that you tailor what you

The Pursuit of Integrity 15

say to be pleasing, inoffensive and possibly self-serving. To be impartial and absolutely truthful, on the other hand, is to have courage—also a part of integrity. As a person of integrity, you will always mean what you say and say only what you mean. This is honest and truthful which pleases God. How do I know that? It is written in Matt. 17:5 that God the Father said, "This is My beloved Son, with whom I am well pleased; listen to Him!"

You see, when you are loyal to the truth over those who are opposed to it or offended by it, then you are being loyal to the character of God; doing what He would do, imitating Christ and being obedient to God who commands us to speak the truth (Eph. 4:25).

As a person of integrity you are both responsible and dependable. These two ingredients are sort of a tandem. If you ignore some responsibilities can you think of yourself as a responsible person? Are you dependable? Well certainly not in the sense you want to be. Part of integrity is being consistent, thorough or complete in your life. The greatest responsibility of all time is stated in Matt. 22:37, which says, "You shall love the Lord your God with all your heart, and with all your soul, and with all your mind. This is the greatest and foremost commandment." So who do you think God sees as the person of integrity with whom He is pleased? Right. The one who loves Him. My friend, please don't miss the point here. God created everyone, so what I am writing about here applies to everyone He created. This is not religion. This is reality. Integrity loves reality.

The measure of integrity in your life is found right here in this command (Matt. 22:37). The extent to which you execute this responsibility IS the extent to which you possess integrity. In addition, let's not overlook the second greatest responsibility given to us. That is to love our neighbor as ourselves. Our neighbors, who are perhaps not so attractive, perhaps because they are obnoxious or unfriendly, are just the ones who provide a check on our integrity. Because God says that if you don't love your neighbor who you can see then you don't love God who you cannot see (1 Jn.4:20-21). How about that!

Let me take you a little farther here to see if you do love your neighbor; a measure of your integrity. The passage is Matt. 5:38-48. Here Jesus simply and profoundly points out that if you only do for others what they do for you, or if you only love those who love you in return, then you fall short of God's standard for real love. He says you are to do good to those who are your enemies! To love those who love you is justice. This is treating people with honesty, fairness and equity. This is morality. But guess what? If this is all you have then you do not have integrity—called "perfect" in verse 48. Furthermore, if you do not go beyond justice, honesty and morality, then you do not love God! (Remember 1 Jn. 4:20-21; Matt. 5:43-48).

Now perhaps you see clearly there is a great difference between man's standards (which are many) and God's standard (which is one). Integrity is God's standard. You might say there is a human or secular integrity; but since it has no value to God, then what value is it? Integrity loves what God loves and values what He values (not man's).

Isaiah said: "For My (Yahweh) thoughts are not your thoughts (loves and values). Nor are your ways (motives and methods) My ways," declares the LORD. For as the heavens are higher than the earth, So are My ways higher than your ways And My thoughts than your thoughts" (55:8-9).

QUALITY OF LIFE

To illustrate love and the behavior of a man of integrity, Jesus told this story in Luke 10:30-37. Note how He made a point of showing that religion is not enough. The priest and the Levite had religion, but not integrity. They did not love God. They loved their religion. Religion and reality differ (see Religion or Life). Reality is what you are on the inside; inside your heart. The true status of your integrity will be revealed by testing, when you are put under pressure or you are challenged to practice what you preach. The priest and the Levites were challenged by this victim of loss and pain. In spite of all their devotion and loyalties to their religion, they failed the integrity test (see The Human Struggle and Tests)! The Samaritan did not hesitate. He saw an opportunity to use his integrity and took it. His giving, compassion, trust and selfless love to the stranger was a reflection of his interior. He passed the integrity test, pleased God and had his integrity strengthened altogether. He placed greater value on integrity than his time, possessions and what others thought. He could not have had any personal love for a stranger in need he had never met. NO, he was motivated by the love in his own integrity, which is an example of God's love for even those who reject Him.

Here are two pertinent passages regarding God's position on your life:

The Lord said to Samuel, ". . . God sees not as man sees, for man looks at the outward appearance, but the Lord looks at the heart" (1 Sam. 16:7).

So guess what God is doing?

"For the eyes of the LORD move to and fro throughout the earth that He may strongly support those whose heart is completely His (full of integrity)" (II Chron. 16:9).

You are given historical examples of men of integrity; real people with real circumstances which Jesus verified while He was here. Three men in particular are selected by God for special mention both in the Old Testament and the New Testament (Ezk. 14:14; Heb. 11:7). They are Noah, Job and Daniel. God had searched their hearts and found unique integrity.

Noah and his family maintained their love for the truth in spite of the whole world's disagreement and opposition. This took great faith, great confidence in God and courage toward man—all qualities of integrity (see Gen. 7-9). God was so aware of Job's integrity that He seemed to be proud of it when He called Satan's attention to Job. Note in Job 1:8 how the NASB version translates God's definition of integrity:

"For there is no one like him on the earth, a blameless and upright man, fearing God and turning away from evil."

Then as a proud Father, God begins the testing of Job's integrity. Job suffered great loss, as recorded in chapter two. Note in verse three how God was watching Job's integrity. The LORD said to Satan, "And he (Job) still holds fast his integrity . . ." See how integrity protects you? You still have loss but you are not destroyed by it. Note that loss or gain is not a measure of integrity, and integrity is the solution to the potential ill effects of loss and gain! (Of course, many do not agree. See verse 9). The response of integrity to loss or gain is found in verse 21: "The Lord gave and the Lord has taken away. Blessed be the name of the Lord."

God's response to Job in verse 22: "Through all this Job did not sin nor did he blame God."

Job's integrity response to additional testing is found in 2:10: "Shall we indeed accept good from God and not accept adversity?"

God's response is in verse 10: "In all this Job did not sin with his lips."

You see, the antithesis to these examples is this. If you hold on to what you have (people, stuff, or money), then you will not be willing to help your neighbor (like the Samaritan) or you might complain if you lose it (unlike Job). If you are a possessor, or a complainer over loss, then you have an integrity problem (see Contentment). In fact, if you complain at loss, and by that I mean you react with negative emotion or verbal outcry, then you are proving Satan right when he said what he did to God about people who have loss or gain (1:9-11, 2:4-5). Satan, who gave up his integrity long ago, seeks to justify himself by proving that no one else has any integrity either (see *Angelic Conflict*).

He tried again with our third Old Testament historical figure; Daniel. Daniel was tested in extraordinary ways; through loss, the threat of loss, and through great gain, he was enticed to fear, turn away from truth, hide his faith, and exploit his position, not to mention to be proud or arrogant about the great revelations that were given to him. But he did not succumb to any of these tests. He passed all integrity tests to the point where it is recorded for us that God held him in "great esteem" (Dan. 10:11,12,19). Verse 12, in particular, explains to us the frame of mind of Daniel which catapulted him to the position which pleases God, and a position in which God could use Daniel for such special service; a special agent, if you will.

"Do not be afraid, Daniel, for from the first day that you set your heart on understanding and humbling yourself before your God, your words were heard, and I have come in response to your words" (Dan. 10:12).

I hope that as you read, "the first day that you set your heart", you were reminded of the verse I recently used from II Chron. 16:9. Please go back and read it. My friend, God is actively looking for integrity of heart. That is why I am writing this paper; to challenge myself and anyone else to, "set your heart," to be found with this in you, a goal or asset that you cannot lose. How do you get it? I have already given part of the answer and will give more, but note the two qualities in v 12 that moved Daniel ahead. He had a passion to learn the truth ("understanding") and he "humbled himself". Without humility, you will not acknowledge you are ignorant, or that you are wrong about some things, or even that you over-value things that are distractions. This is arrogance.

There were other people of historical integrity. Many are listed in Hebrews 11. The courage, faith and love for the truth of these are commended by God. In fact, He says that because of their great integrity, they will "obtain a better resurrection" (v35). This means that integrity has a positive effect on your future forever!

In spite of the greatness of the examples mentioned, they were too few and far too inadequate to reveal completely the integrity that God wanted to be the role model for His church; His Bride-to-be!

God's plan to bring His own integrity to earth is amazing. How would God obtain a perfect human body which was not contaminated by the sin of Adam; too weak to live the integrity of God?

Step 1: When Adam and Eve sinned, God had already created biological reproduction in them so that more people would come from them.

Step 2: Because they sinned perhaps you would think this sin would destroy any chance of God becoming a man. No, because God is wiser (integrity) than everyone. He thinks ahead! He made sure that the physical genetic factor attached to that sin which would be passed down from generation to generation would not be attached to the woman who had already been created to form the baby.

Step 3: But to the male, He gave the "sin gene", so that a human father for the "Son of Man" would not be possible.

Step 4: Then God intervened in the natural process of things and created a baby by His Spirit, just as He had created Adam years ago by His Spirit (Gen. 2:-7; Lk. 1:34-35).

The Pursuit of Integrity

So He was born from man, therefore called the Son of Man, but also born of God, therefore called the Son of God. The God-Man, Jesus Christ, has revealed the perfect integrity of God to us. The apostle John wrote, "And the Word (God) became flesh, and dwelt among us, and we saw His glory (essence and integrity), glory as of the only begotten from the Father, full of grace and truth" (Jn 1:14), "He (the Son) has revealed Him" (the Father) (v18).

Paul said, "He (Jesus) is the IMAGE of the invisible God, the firstborn of all creation" (Col. 1: 15). "For in Him (the Son) all the fullness of Deity dwells in bodily form . . ." (Col. 2:9).

The writer of Hebrews is very explicit: "And He (Christ) is the radiance of His (Father) glory and the EXACT representation of His (Father's) nature . . ." (Heb. 1:3). The words "glory" and "nature" are synonyms - their meanings are similar. And so they are synonyms of integrity (see Addendum). This means you could read the verse in this way, "Christ is the radiance of the Father's integrity and the exact representation of His integrity". Glory and nature both include God's integrity, which is composed, remember, of four parts of His glory. These four are His righteousness, justice, truth and love. (You should learn these in this order).

So completely did Jesus Christ model the integrity of God that He Himself said, "He who has seen Me has seen the Father . . ." (Jn. 14:9). A most poignant point here is this. Integrity is not something that can be defined by man because man does not have it in his nature. Righteousness, justice, truth and love are not in his nature; not in the absolute sense or any sense complete enough so he can establish the standard for what integrity is. Therefore, God had to reveal His integrity to us so we could know how to live. He has done that; now it is your responsibility and privilege to pursue that integrity.

Our enemy does not want you to pursue integrity. I refer you to Genesis 3. Adam and Eve, our parents, knew only good from and about God, their Creator. Satan's scheme to destroy that was to suggest to them, to lie to them that what they knew and what they were was not enough. (A suggestion that God was withholding something necessary from them!) Satan made them think that they would know more, including evil, and they would be more like God. They listened to the wrong source and therefore got the wrong information. Now see how the tables have turned. Our parents knew perfectly about God and were in perfect relationship with Him. Now we, their offspring, live in need to correct our thinking about Him and get that integrity they lost; learn it and live it, developing a relationship with Him that pleases Him. They stepped into darkness and we need to step out of it. But thanks to God's integrity, we can do so and, in fact, are commanded to do so.

"And do not be conformed to this world, but be transformed by the renewing of your mind, so that you may prove what the will of God is, that which is good and pleasing and perfect" (Rom. 12:2). "Good, pleasing and perfect" are synonyms for what?

Think about the first Adam and the second Adam (Jesus Christ) (Rom. 5:14). God gave them both people in their lives who they could love and care for; to whom they had responsibility and obligation. Yet in the case of the old Adam, it was not sin against Eve that brought death and a damaged relationship, it was sin against God. Then in the case of the new Adam, it was not complete love and concern for people that qualified Christ to be our Savior, but it was complete obedience to God the Father and a sustained right relationship with Him.

The point is, my friend, that right relationship with God is where integrity is. And it can only be right when this relationship is the most important thing in your life. Let me put it this way;

The Pursuit of Integrity

you can be the best wife, mother, father, worker or citizen; above the rest and outstanding. BUT, if these priorities crowd out and supersede the very reason you were created, that is, God's priority for you, then you are actually a failure. You don't feel or think you are a failure, but that is because you are meeting your own goals; goals which even are agreeable to those around you who are also doing the same thing with their lives. You are measuring yourself by your own standards, therefore you approve of yourself. Integrity does not do this. Integrity is constantly seeking to adjust your life priorities to what pleases God first, not people. Do you think Jesus Christ lived His life to please people? He is your role model; the model of integrity. He did what was best for people, children and adults, those He knew and loved and those He had never met. That is, He did exactly what pleased God. Remember what God spoke from heaven about Him? "This is My beloved Son, in whom I am well pleased" (Matt. 3:17). He does think the same thing about you, if you also have His integrity. How do I know that? I have already answered this question (Job 1:8). " . . . God knows your hearts" (Lk. 16:15; I Chron. 28:9).

Real Integrity

Loving God is your greatest responsibility! You can reject it, fight it, deny it or ignore it, but just like all other truth, you cannot get rid of it You cannot eject God from your life and claim to have integrity. You have then only developed your own self-satisfying complacency, approved of by others of course, but in the reality of all truth and before God's eyes, you have destroyed your own integrity. You have substituted what you could have had with a pseudo self-esteem, which is the definition of arrogance!

There is human viewpoint and divine viewpoint. There is human good and divine good. There is human solution and divine solution. Then, there is human integrity and divine integrity. All that is divine in these categories is found in the Bible. All that is human comes from people and makes up what the Bible calls the "world" or "worldliness". Conflict throughout the Bible itself is due to the contradiction between that which is human and that which is divine. God rejects ALL that is human because it is inadequate (I Cor. 13:1-3). All good, all integrity and solution must have right motive, right method, right love, right perception, right faith and right choice. This brings the good up for the Divine stamp of approval. Yet there still remains the need for you to be "walking" in the light, walking in the truth, walking in love and walking in the Spirit. Only now does your integrity, your good, and your life meet God's approval. Now He is pleased.

Real integrity does not live a life of duplicity (hypocrisy). So many settle into duplicity because it has social approval. Duplicity does not create conflict with people simply because many you know are doing the same things. For example, you may call yourself a Catholic, a Presbyterian or an Adventist, while at the same time you admit, at least to yourself, that you do not believe some of the doctrines taught by the group with which you identify, to which you give your time, energy, and money.

Worse yet, you may call yourself a Christian, a follower and believer in Jesus Christ, but reject things that He teaches. You might reject that He is God, or that He is the only way of salvation, or that He has to be the first love of your life. To claim to be something you are not is commonly called hypocrisy, lying or pretense. Why do many of you do this? Why are so many comfortable with living in a state of irrational thinking or double thinking (a violation of your I). Why create a false impression of yourself by yourself?

This behavior, in effect, is a failure of your integrity; it is not honest. There is not advantage in identifying yourself with something you don't fully believe in. This is loss; bad loss. And not only do you lose what you have, you fail to gain what you could have; a more perfect integrity. There are many integrity failures recorded for you to learn from. For example, Pilate was a man of patience and perception, but he loved the power. Judas was a man who walked the walk and talked the talk, but he loved the money. Peter was a man who loved the Lord, but he denied Him because he loved his life. Another great example comes from the story of the wayward son in Luke 15:11-32. The older brother was not greedy, worked hard, was obedient, moral and dependable, but when challenged with grace, he failed. You could sum him up this way: He (v. 25-32) had righteousness, had justice and had truth, but he failed to love his brother.

Integrity is only real when it is complete or whole, just like the Latin word "integer" to which it is related. Integer means whole or one. Do you ever feel like there is something missing in your life? If so, check out the addendum. And remember that the short definition of integrity is love for the truth. If you do this then you will eventually, and simultaneously qualify in every item listed in the Addendum.

Real integrity is proven by the challenges that come its way. You will be challenged to fear loss, to have double standards, to demand justice, to hold grudges, to be controlled by what people think, to overvalue justice, people and appearance while undervaluing integrity, truth, honesty and humility. Integrity meets all these challenges with courage toward people and confidence in God. Integrity corrects its value system so that all things are put into proper priority, ensuring reaching right goals.

MOTIVATION FOR INTEGRITY

How can you get motivated to pursue something which will put you in contrast and conflict with many other people? This means you will have a very different set of values than the rest of the world. You will be going against the grain as we say. You may be ridiculed, misunderstood, isolated or rejected even by those you are related to.

On the other hand, you will gain something that will insulate you from all this negativity. Since you no longer overvalue what others say or think, then you are unaffected by them. Your internal satisfaction with your integrity gives you all the contentment you need. In addition, you know that applause, appeal, attractiveness, wealth, power, status and stuff can all be lost; it has limited value and you have no ultimate control over it. You cannot control what people think about you, but you can control what you value and you can control your pursuit of integrity. You can also maintain it and never lose it should you be so motivated.

Motivation comes from knowledge of the value of the goal. This has to be learned. Here is where the push-pull principle comes to bear. Having learned about integrity, you find it attractive, therefore you are PULLED to it. If you don't find it desirable and you prefer to join the greater society of the miserable then once your failures come along with disappointment, frustration and discouragement then you may, hopefully, feel a PUSH to go another direction in your life. The pain of a bad value system and wrong choices will motivate you to change. Change is absolutely necessary. Here is the purpose of all evil, bad and pain in your life. That is, not to create guilt in you because you may not even be responsible for it, but all you dislike is designed to push you toward the good; the integrity of soul that will grant you security, stability, contentment and joy in spite of any negative circumstances. The changes you make in your value system to get the integrity you need comes with a cost.

THE COST of INTEGRITY

The costs are great. Believe it or not, a lot of people, if not most, prefer to worry, stress-out, negatively emote, and smother themselves with an endless number of details that amount to nothing!

You will have to give all this up. You will have to give up being discouraged, being felt sorry for, being pacified, being bored and selfishly sensitive. You can no longer love just some people or be friendly to just some people. You will have to love everyone.

You will have to give up a lot of short-term pleasure and fun. As well as the pseudo-security which comes from money and people. And since integrity is more important to you, you will not be able to use people or use any double standards to get what most people value.

Now here is the really big cost. You will no longer be able to justify yourself when you are wrong and you will not be able to hold on to injustices that have come your way. I told you, integrity costs plenty! You recognize we all have faults and make mistakes.

Real Integrity

Sometimes we all have integrity failures. Therefore, it is not a loss on your part to take responsibility for any error on your part. In fact, you don't lose face, you gain integrity every time you take responsibility for your actions. Confession and forgiveness are the keys to sustaining a relationship. Arrogance refuses to confess or forgive. On the other hand, integrity takes every opportunity to do both because this is how it builds itself up.

Remember righteousness, justice, truth and love? Well, righteousness and justice makes you AWARE of the need for confession and forgiveness. Then, confession is a function of truth and forgiveness is a function of love. (Real love includes grace). In other words, Truth confesses and Love forgives.

In addition to all the values and virtues I have listed so far, be sure to know that NO person of integrity worth his "salt" would be short on gratitude. Col. 2:7 says to be "overflowing with gratitude", or as we say, an attitude of gratitude. In this state of mind you don't complain about what you don't have, but you are thankful for what you do have. Neither do you take the credit for it, but you give thanks always to the One who gave it to you, even if He takes it from you (see *Contentment*).

Let me be a little more thorough about confession. The first part of confession involves yourself. It simply means that you are honest with yourself, so that you take responsibility for your error. Next, there is the greatest and second greatest commandments (responsibilities) to consider; namely, God and your neighbor. If you sinned against God, then you will need to confess to Him. David said in Ps. 32:5, "I acknowledged my sin to You, And my iniquity I did not hide; I said, 'I will confess my transgressions to the Lord'...."

Then if you have sinned against someone, you should do likewise; ask their forgiveness. Remember that even you with integrity will have failures. This is how it is kept intact, that is, by taking responsibility for your failures. James said in 5:16, "Confess your sins to one another . . . ."

Confession does not make you a weak person, it makes you an honest, humble, responsible, strong person.

Forgiveness is the other side of this valuable coin. It is similar to confession, except that you do not forgive God. Instead, He forgives you. You forgive yourself because God does; even if your neighbor will not forgive you. Why? Because of integrity. Forgiveness is a part of integrity. God does it and you are to be like Him, not like your neighbor. So, you forgive yourself, you forgive your neighbor and you accept God's forgiveness. David went on to say in Ps. 32:5, "And you (God) forgave the guilt of my sin".

The apostle John records this promise from our Father in 1 John 1:9, "If we confess our sins, He (God) is faithful and just to forgive us our sins and to cleanse us from all unrighteousness." This means that confession, and only confession, is necessary for complete forgiveness. Don't you dare add anything to this. If you do you will destroy your own integrity!

Now consider people to people again. Jesus said to pray, "Our Father . . . forgive us our sins, as we also forgive those who have sinned against us" (paraphrase of Matt. 6:2; Lk. 11:4). Do you require or demand something from your neighbor before you will forgive them? Your friend, your relative or your spouse? Do you require a payback, a payoff or an eye for an eye? If you do then how do you expect to be forgiven yourself? If you think God requires these things from you when you confess, then you don't know God at all. You need to read Matt. 5:38-48. He is a God of love that forgives freely. This is called GRACE (see God, Grace and the Gift of Grace).

"Then Peter came and said to Him, 'Lord, how often shall my brother sin against me and I forgive him? Up to seven times?'

Jesus said to him, 'I do not say to you up to seven times, but up to seventy times seven'" (Matt. 18:21-22).

Now does this sound like the offender was required to say "I'll never do it again", or make any other concession or promise? It is clear from this passage what God will do and what you should do when any confession is made; forgive, forgive and FORGIVE.

The greatest demonstration of God's grace forgiveness, second only to the cross itself, is His relationship with Israel. He chose them, but they would not choose Him and still do not. He gave them information, leaders and all they needed, even though He knew they would rebel and even reject their own Messiah; God Himself. This is grace. If you want to have integrity, get to know grace and practice it all the time.

A relationship without thoroughgoing confession and forgiveness is doomed. It is low on integrity. It will consist of conflict, contest and possibly contact. Do not delay confession and forgiveness. Do not compromise. Do not cover up. Do not minimize your responsibility. Integrity LOVES to confess and forgive. Integrity LOVES to be corrected by anyone at anytime because it wants to be true and accurate! Be corrected, be advised, be taught, be judged and be made complete, perfect and noble (see Addendum).

THE EXTREMES OF INTEGRITY

Extreme value calls for extreme measure. Remember that pursuing integrity is done by pursuing the Person of integrity, so when Jesus said that you would have to love Him more than even your own relatives (Matt. 10:34-39) possibly resulting in division from them, then this is extreme. He said to find His life, which is integrity, you would have to lose your own (v39)! Also found in Lk. 14:25-33, where you read in addition to the extreme of total commitment to the Person of Integrity you are required "to give up all your possessions." This means that you can no longer be possessive; obsessed with what you have. This, of course, is why integrity does not lose it emotionally when anything or anyone becomes loss!

In the extreme pursuit of integrity you will not be distracted by many things that are traditional or even expected by others. For example, read the companion passage of Matt. 8:19-22 and Lk. 9:57-60. The most extreme example, I believe, the Lord gave of the value of integrity was when in Mk. 9:43-47 He said that if your own hand, foot or eye hinders your pursuit in some way, then get rid of it! How extreme is this? But remember, you will lose all those parts anyway. It is only your integrity that you can take with you (called "salt" in v50). And you will take it with you, however small or great it may be.

SUMMARY OF INTEGRITY

You can personally define and decide what is pleasing, attractive, pleasant, appealing and even admirable to yourself, but it is God Who decides and defines what integrity is. It is He who sets the standards that measure your integrity and therefore only He can reveal what these standards are and only He can judge each of us fairly by these standards.

Your responsibility is to learn God's integrity, pursue it, imitate it and take it with you when you leave. Don't forget this phrase: Value what He values and love what He loves. With this modus operandi (MO) you will not react to unfair, overbearing, arrogant and insensitive people. You are not shaken by loss or the threat of loss because you now value MUCH MORE that thing you cannot lose; integrity.

When you value integrity you will have an entirely different opinion of all negatives that come your way, even if they are not real. Your response will be different. Things that would have irritated, aggravated or frustrated you no longer do because you

Real Integrity

are not on the defense, not in a contest, not overvaluing fair treatment, pleasant behavior or gain you might deserve. These things are normal, but not priority. Priority is your integrity, which is kept intact and strengthened when you are patient, kind, gentle, forgiving, honest and content in all circumstances. This is the stability and strength that is at the core of integrity.

The cost of integrity is a loss and this loss is two-fold: Loss of value of the things you overvalue. You will lose the value you now give relationships, material possessions, food, entertainment, sex, money, prestige, status, other people's opinion of you, leisure and the approval of others. This is a great loss, but not a total loss because these things are not terminated; they are only adjusted in value relative to your growing love for truth, God, people, honesty, humility, confession, forgiveness, right motive, and integrity.

The second loss you pay is one that will be quite painful to many. You may think you cannot live without something or someone. You may think you cannot live without revenge, criticism, sympathy, self-pity, stress, anxiety, worry, fear and especially, brace yourself, complaining! I am being facetious, but for a reason. That reason is to provoke you to realize there is life without negativity, weakness, stress and fear, and a life when even though you may be a victim, you can maintain a position of strength rather than a position of frustration, discouragement or disappointment.

In closing, the cost of building and maintaining integrity is great, BUT the payoff is astronomical. So great is the difference of the life experience of the one with it and the one without it, the Bible uses the extreme descriptives of day and night, light and darkness, death and LIFE!

Addendum

BIBLICAL SYNONYMS AND METAPHORS FOR INTEGRITY
(Taken from the NIV, NASB and KJV translations)

1. Root — (Luke 8:13)
2. Good Tree — (Luke 6:43)
3. Salt — (Luke 14:34)
4. Light — (Matt. 6:22)
5. Mature — (James 1:4)
6. Fullness — (Eph. 3:19)
7. Godliness — (II Tim. 4:8)
8. Holiness — (I Peter 1:16)
9. Man of Truth — (Matt. 22:16)
10. Highly Esteemed — (Dan. 10:11, 19)
11. Complete — (Rev. 3:2; II Cor. 13:9, 11)
12. Humble — (Dan. 10:12)
13. Wise — (Matt. 7:24)
14. Full of Love — (James 5:11)
15. Full of Faith — (Acts 6:5)
16. Stable — (II Peter 1:12)
17. Honest and Good Heart — (Luke. 8:15)
18. Good Eyes — (Matt. 6:22)
19. A Perfect Heart — (I Chron. 12:38)
20. Uprighteousness — (I Chron. 29:17; Ps. 119:7; Job 1:1, 8)
21. Truthful — (John. 3:33)
22. Righteousness — (Ezk. 14:20)
23. Glory — (John. 1:14; Heb. 1:3)
24. Virtue — (Col. 3:12-14)
25. Proven Character — (Rom. 5:4)
26. Noble Character — (Ruth 3:11; Prov. 12:4, 31:10; Acts 17:11)
27. Perfect
28. Noble Minded

29. Integrity (Matt. 5:48; Job 1:1)
30. Overflowing w/ (Heb. 1:3)
    Gratitude (Ps. 15:2)
31. A Man of Integrity (Col. 2:7; I Thess. 5:18)
32. Fearing God (Matt. 22:16)
33. Hating Evil (Job 1:1, 8)
34. Strong (Job 1:1, 8; Rom. 12:9)
35. Content (Rom. 15:1)
36. Joyful (II Cor. 12:10; Phil. 4:11-12)
37. Relaxed Mental (I Thess. 5:16)
    Attitude (Heb. 4:10-11; Phil. 4: 11-12)
38. Sanctified (John 17:17)
39. Impartial (Gal. 2:6)
40. Patient (Col. 3:12)
41. Great (Job 1:3)
42. Blameless (Job 1:1, 8)

Test or Contest

My personal motto which I wrote for myself goes like this:

LIFE is a TEST
NOT a CONTEST

I use this motto daily. It is DIVINE VIEWPOINT. To introduce this subject, here is a partial list of pertinent verses.

James 4:1 "What cause fights and quarrels among you?"

4:11 ". . . do not slander one another."

4:16 ". . . you boast and brag . . . is evil."

5:9 "Don't grumble against each other . . . you will be judged."

Gal. 5:26 "Let us not become conceited (arrogant), provoking and envying each other."

1 Pet. 3:9 "Do not repay evil with evil or insult with insult . . ."

These passages speak of CONFLICT between people. Conflict is a CONTEST (see motto above). Contest says . . . "I am right, you are wrong. I am better than you are. You did me wrong. My anger is justified." You hurt me. My whining and self-pity are justified. These are CONTESTS. It doesn't matter who starts the contest. BLAMING the one who starts it is simply an EXCUSE to participate!

If this is your life, then you are a SLAVE to the behaviors of others as well as a SLAVE to your own 'FEELINGS'. You are immature and furthermore you are DECEIVED about yourself.

"If anyone thinks he is something when he is nothing, he DECEIVES himself." Gal. 6:3

Self-deception is the RESULT of self-importance, self-justification, self-promotion, self-righteousness, and self-absorption. If you think and live like life is a CONTEST then this is where you are—in self-absorption. This MENTAL state of mind is deceptive. You are convinced you are RIGHT to 'feel' the way you do; after all, consider the way people treat you (or someone has treated you) and consider how important you are. Living several 'notches' above others you are quick to see their flaws AND to point them out—for their benefit of course!

I call this 'living in relativity' or COMPARISON LIVING. Your selfworth is DEPENDENT on the opinion of OTHERS about you, you MUST defend yourself, PROVE you are right, SHOW what you know, and WIN every CONTEST.

"We do not dare to classify or COMPARE ourselves with some who COMMEND THEMSELVES. When they MEASURE themselves and COMPARE themselves with themselves, they are NOT wise." "For it is NOT the one who commends himself who is APPROVED, but the one whom the LORD commends." II Cor. 10:12,18.

Back to the book of James:

"What CAUSES fights (contests) and quarrels (contests) among you?

Don't they come from your DESIRES that BATTLE within you?" 4:1

Key words here are DESIRES and BATTLE. These desires struggle for control of your life, to win control over your soul. What are these desires? (I refer you to the entire context of James 4:1-12) They are desires of SELF-SEEKING behavior. 'Desires' that drive us to seek ATTENTION, APPLAUSE, APPROBATION, and ADVANCEMENT. That is, to be BETTER THAN someone else, to be right, to be in control, even to demand JUSTICE for self.

"You quarrel and fight (v2b)." Why? To WIN! If you have to STRUGGLE to get your way or prove someone wrong, then you are NOT the winner, you ARE the loser. You are a LOSER!

The basic MENTAL attitude SIN here is ARROGANCE. Why? Because arrogance is always right, needs to be right, to be on top, and will quarrel, fight, argue, complain, manipulate, and control to get there. Look at Gal. 5:26 again.

"Let us NOT become conceited (arrogant), provoking (conflict) and envying (contest) each other."

Notice the obvious SYMPTOMS of arrogance—MENTAL and VERBAL antagonism with others.

This behavior is a life of CONTEST with your 'neighbor' (as opposed to 'loving' your neighbor). It is a life of STRESS instead of REST, and a life of ME, MYSELF, and I. This mental attitude does not have respect for the RIGHT of others to make their own choices (live and let live). This is also arrogance, that is, FORCING your choices on another.

"God OPPOSES the proud (arrogant), but gives grace to the humble." James 4:6

God hates arrogance so much that He actually works against those who are arrogant. He NEVER forces Himself on anyone. Even if He knows it would be for their OWN GOOD! He never violates anyone's volition and He OPPOSES those who do (v.6).

Believers do have a conflict (contest) but NOT with people. Our conflict is with the "flesh" (sin nature within each of us).

"For the sinful nature DESIRES what is CONTRARY to the Spirit, and the Spirit what is CONTRARY to the sinful nature. They are in CONFLICT with each other . . ." Gal. 5:17

A second 'front' on which we are in conflict is the spirit world.

"For our STRUGGLE is NOT against flesh and blood (people) but against . . ." Eph. 6:12 Read this passage.

More will be said about these two 'fronts' in other chapters but for now notice from the two verses above that ONLY those with a spiritual life—BORN AGAIN—have a contest. NEVER with people. OUR contest is with the 'sin nature' and the antagonistic spirit world! The conflict of UNBELIEVERS is with people, in fact, this is their ONLY 'front'. Therefore IF you are a believer and you CHOOSE to argue, quarrel, compete, and struggle with others, then you APPEAR to be an unbeliever and you are on the WRONG front.

"Each one should TEST his OWN actions. Then he can take pride in himself, without COMPARING himself to somebody else . . ." Gal. 6:4

You are to FOCUS on your OWN behavior, NOT on the behavior of the other. If you focus on their behavior you will REACT, allowing them to CONTROL you. If you go on 'COMPARING' (verse above) yourself to others, then you are in 'comparison living'—living in relativity. WAKE UP! Do not be DECEIVED. Who is deceived? The one who lives for self, believing he is FREE from restraint, free to react, argue, quarrel, slander, and justify self WITHOUT CONSEQUENCES.

"Do not be deceived: God CANNOT be mocked. A man reaps what he sows." Gal. 6:7

The behavior of the believer is REQUIRED to be INDEPENDENT of others. If you do this, then you can take "pride in yourself" (see v 4 above). This is true SELF-ESTEEM.

Test or Contest

BUT if you are a 'contest type', into comparison living, then your self-esteem is COUNTERFEIT. Counterfeit self-esteem is arrogance . . . insecure, quarreling, hypersensitive and suspicious!

To try to build self-esteem on the misfortune of others is at best shallow and stupid. To see yourself as better than someone—anyone else—is NOT to SEE yourself at all. This is BLIND arrogance (or self-deception). The blind and the deceived bump into each other all the time!

Paul had to remind such people that there are NO special people, NO social elite, and NO racial or ethnic superiority. See Gal. 3:28. Divine viewpoint, the MENTAL attitude of the spiritually mature, says that God LOVES everyone equally, indeed, He is NOT a respecter of persons. If you feel ANY degree of superiority based on your race, social, economic, or physical status (including the poor, disabled, or ugly) then you are OUT of line . . . for happiness, but IN line for misery, stress, and discipline. Mental attitude sins WILL lead to verbal sins. What does God consider the WORST sins?

"These are six things the Lord HATES, seven that are DETESTABLE to Him:

haughty eyes, (arrogance)	mental
a lying tongue	verbal
hands that shed innocent blood	overt
a heart that devises wicked schemes	mental
feet that are quick to rush into evil	mental
a false witness who pours out lies	verbal
and a man who stirs up dissension among brothers." Prov. 6:16-19	verbal

Please notice the priorities of divine viewpoint. Only ONE OVERT sin is named, that is, murder. The other six are MENTAL and VERBAL! God's Word is full of this emphasis. Your spiritual life is NOT what you do but what you THINK. For a partial disclosure of this doctrine, see the addendum.

"But if you harbor envy (mental attitude sin) . . . in your heart, do not boast . . . or deny the truth (verbal sin)." Js. 3:14

"If anyone . . . does not keep a rein on his tongue (verbal sins), he DECEIVES himself." Js. 1:26

Principle: If you CHOOSE to live your life as a contest, you WILL have mental attitude sins. If you JUSTIFY these sins -listed on the addendum, you are DENYING them. Denial leads to SELF-DECEPTION.

In denial, your PLAN is to be treated fairly. This is your expectation. Your FOCUS is on how OTHERS treat you. Sensitive to the behavior of others toward you, you constantly monitor their behavior, and when your standard (expectation) is not met, you REACT. What are the symptoms of reaction? See the addendum—all of it!

God's PLAN is that we FOCUS on Him (not on others or ourselves). To love Him and learn about Him. In His plan we WILL be mistreated.
EXPECT mistreatment.
When it comes, do this:

"Be completely humble and gentle; be patient, bearing with one another in LOVE." Eph. 4:2

Do you think God is in heaven REACTING to every insult and sin that comes His way? Of course not. His INTEGRITY won't allow it. This Integrity is to be seen in you every opportunity (mistreatment) you get!

" . . . be made NEW in the ATTITUDE of your MIND, and put on the NEW SELF, created to be LIKE God . . ." Eph, 4:23-24.

Job was a man who experienced a degree of UNDESERVED sufferings that was extreme. (See Job Chapter 1). While under this "mistreatment", he refused to COMPLAIN or BLAME (v. 20-22). His wife (a contest type) said to him "Do you still hold on to your INTEGRITY? Curse God and die! (Job 2:9).

She had the right question, the same question we should ask ourselves. Will we maintain integrity (strength of character)? When you are provoked, challenged, misunderstood, mistreated, abused, violated, victimized, ignored, slandered, intimidated, scolded, and guess what? Flattered! REMEMBER . . . Life is a TEST . . . NOT a CONTEST.

The Pursuit of INTEGRITY

MENTAL ATTITUDE SINS lead to VERBAL SINS

"Man looks at the outward appearance but the Lord looks at the HEART." I Sam. 16:7

Fear: II Tim. 1:7, Matt. 6:25-34 Prov. 3:25, Ps. 32:8
Guilt: (unconfessed sin) I Jn. 1:9,
Self-pity, Vanity: Rom. 12:16

Arrogance: Jer. 49:16, I Cor. 4:6-7, Lk. 18:9, I Cor. 1:19, Rom. 12:3, 16, Gal. 6:3
Hatred: Col. 3:8, Titus 3:3, 3:2
Anger: Eph. 4:31, Col. 3:8, Lk. 15:28
Bigotry, Prejudice: I Cor. 4:6 Col. 3:8
Contempt: Rom. 14:10, Col. 3:8
Busy-body: I Thess. 4:11, Jn. 8:4-5
Manipulation: I Thess. 4:6
Divisive: I Cor. 3:1-3, 11: 18-19

Jealousy: Gal. 5:20, Lk. 15:29-30
Best example - Saul, I Sam. 18
Petty: Titus 3:3
Greed: Eph. 5:3, Col. 3:5

Self-centered: Col. 2:18, Titus 3:3

Malice, Cruelty: Eph. 4:31, II Cor. 10:10
Self-righteous (fault-finding): Lk. 18:9, Col. 2:20-23, Jn. 8:6, Matt. 23:25, 28
Implacable, 'demand' syndrome: Prov. 21:19-ff

Creature worship, Approbation: Ps. 73: 1-9, I Cor. 7:23, I Thess. 2:4, Gal. 1:10

"His (Job's) wife said to him, Are you still holding on to your INTEGRITY?" Curse God and die." Job 2:9

Complaining/whining: Prov. 18:12, Phil. 2:14, I Cor. 10:10
Self-justification: Lk. 10:29-ff, 16:15
Self-absorption ('hurt' syndrome): II Tim. 3:2, I Cor. 13: 4-5, Gal. 6:3
Self-justification, Self-promotion: Lk. 18:9-14, Lk. 16:15, II Cor. 10:10, 18

Abuse: Gal. 5:20, Col. 3:8, I Pet. 3:9
Vilification: Eph. 4:31, Lk. 15:29-30

Malign: Gal. 5:15, Col. 3:8, Titus 3:2

Character assination: Eph. 4:31
Gossip: I Tim. 3-11, II Cor. 12:20-21
Divisive: Titus 3:10-11
Taking sides: II Cor. 12: 20-21, Gal. 5:20, Titus 3:2
Slander: II Cor. 12:20-21, Eph. 4:31, Lk. 15:30, Col. 3:8
Self-absorption: Lk. 18:9-14

Lying: Eph. 4:29, Jer. 9:5, Col. 3:9, 1 Pet. 3:10
Blaming: II Cor. 12:20-21, Gal. 5:6, Job 1:21-22
Rude, Harsh speech: Gal. 5:20, 22, Eph.4:29
Self-justification, Judging: Gal. 6:7, Lk. 16:15, Lk. 10:29, 18:11-12, I Cor. 4: 3-5, Rom. 14: 4, 13
Complaining, Whining: Jude 16, Phil. 2:11, I Cor. 10:10

Flattery: Ps. 12:2-4, Job 32:21-22, Jude 16, Gal. 6:4
Revenge: Rom. 12:17-20, I Thess. 5:15
Reverse arrogance, Pseudo humility: Col. 21:18, 23.

Frustration: Prov. 21:19-ff

Hypocrisy, Insincerity, Deception: Gal. 2:12-14 6:12-13, Matt. 7:5 Jer. 9:8,6, In. 8:5-6

Lust, Envy: Gal. 5:21, 26, 19, Col. 3:5
Double standard: Js. 4:8, Js. 1:8
Retaliation: Rom. 12: 14-20, 1 Pet. 3: 8-9

'Victim' syndrome. (Arrogance manifested in weakness-form of sublimation)
'Dirty' talk: Eph. 5:4

Judging: Matt. 7:15, Rom. 14: 4,10

Self- Esteem (SE)

How do you feel about yourself? Are you happy with your self, confident, and secure? If you are, then you have SELF-ESTEEM. Synonyms for self-esteem are self-confidence, self-worth, and self-competence. What is the source of self-esteem? I am listing six common sources here. The "6A's":

1. Approval
2. Approbation
3. Achievement
4. Attention
5. Advancement
6. Admiration

These sources of self-esteem (SE) are popular, traditional, and represent what the MAJORITY thinks. These six represent the HUMAN VIEWPOINT about how to build SE. When I say the majority of people depend on the 6A source, I mean 90-95% of people!

A MINORITY of people, 5 to 10%, have learned DIVINE VIEWPOINT which says the 6A source can only build COUNTERFEIT SE. A counterfeit can convince you and others but cannot hold up under pressure and is always dependent on MORE of the 6A source.

Have you ever heard something about someone and then found out later that what you heard was not accurate? Happens all the time. In fact, there may be someone telling something inaccurate about you right now! How would you feel about that?

Should you find out this is true how would you respond . . . or react? Perhaps you would be HURT or get ANGRY, or worse, you would try to get even. If this describes the way you would react, then you have POOR SE, no self-esteem, or counterfeit SE. My professional designation is EDS—esteem deficiency syndrome.

The 6A's are NOT sources of true SE because they are EXTERNAL sources and they are PEOPLE DEPENDENT. Real SE is INTERNAL (from your own integrity) and is God dependent. You can not build SE on relationships with people . . . for many reasons: they don't have the necessary integrity, they are unreliable, unstable, and unfair. ONLY on your relationship with God can you build REAL SE. ONLY He has COMPLETE integrity. He is eternal, stable, and dependable. He LOVES you at ALL times and under all circumstances (Rom. 8:38-39).

The first and greatest commandment (your first responsibility in life) is to LOVE GOD with all your heart, soul, and mind (Matt. 22:36-37). When you love God like this you will have rapport with Him. This rapport creates true SE. You are now confident and poised NOT because of some merit badge you have won or because of some people you know to be impressed with you. You are secure and stable because you have an intimate relationship with the God of the universe!

How do you get to this point? Believe in Jesus Christ. Study His life. He is our role model of SE. Even His enemies recognized the greatness of His SE! (One reason they were jealous of Him)!

The religious Pharisees (His opposition) said to Jesus, "Teacher, we know you are a man of integrity and that you teach the way of God in accordance with the truth. You aren't swayed by men, because you pay NO attention to who they are" (Matt. 22:15-16).

Jesus was free and independent from the opinion, flattery, or commentary of others. This IS role-model behavior. This is great stability, this true self-esteem came to Him through His relationship with His Father, through His sense of purpose,

Self-Esteem

and His destiny. Note in these few verses–RELATIONSHIP, PURPOSE & DESTINY (RPD).

"My food," said Jesus, "is to do the WILL of HIM who sent me and to finish HIS work" (Jn. 4:34, 16:28).

". . . for I know where I came from and where I am going" (Jn. 8:14).

". . . and that He (Jesus) had come from God and was returning to God . . . so He washed His disciples feet" (Jn. 13:1-5).

> P1. True self-esteem PROMOTES humility, because it FREES you from the opinion of others.

Read Matthew 22:16 above again: "a man of integrity" is a person who values the TRUTH (God's will and plan) ABOVE the opinions and opposition of anyone; he is not distracted by people. He gives his "attention" (v16) NOT to people but to God.

Jesus ignored and rejected the 6A sources. When you are building RPD, the 6A source can become a DISTRACTION to you. This is why, "Jesus would NOT entrust Himself to them, for He knew all men". He did NOT need "MAN'S TESTIMONY ABOUT MAN" (the 6A source), for He knew what was in a man (the lust for the 6A source) (Jn. 2:24- 25).

Also, John 5:33 ". . . NOT that I (Jesus) accept human testimony (6A)". John 5:41 "I (Jesus) do NOT accept praise (6A) from men."

Read Genesis 3:1-7. This is the first Biblical example of appeal to the 6A source (Eve's) for the purpose of self-promotion. Eve chose to advance herself to counterfeit SE rather than comply with God's plan (RPD) for her life.

Colossians 3:17, 23 teaches you. "whatever you do, work at it with all your heart, as working for the Lord, NOT for men."

(Only those who prefer 6A do it "for men".)

> P2. Living for God, under His authority, motivated by love for Him, with a view to spending eternity with Him is the formula for true SE.

Jesus Christ had NO interest in winning the approval of others or winning the applause of others (see 6A). He said, "I have brought you glory on earth by completing the work you gave me to do." John 17:4 is a statement of RPD, which is the antithesis of 6A. Why? Because 6A is dependent on people. Review it. Whereas Jesus Christ, the living epitome of SE, was ONLY dependent on and always focused on the Father.

> P3. It is not important what people think or say about me. It is important what my Father thinks about me.

2 Cor. 10:18, "For it is not the one who commends himself (counterfeit self-esteem) who is approved, but the one whom the Lord commends (true self-esteem)".

Lk. 16:15, "What is highly valued among men (6A) is detestable in God's sight".

Matt. 22:16, "You aren't swayed (a slave to the opinion of others) by men, because you pay NO attention to who they are" (focused on RPD).

1 Cor. 4:3-4, "I care very little if I am judged (approved, applauded, see 6A, or the opposite) by you or by any human court. It is the Lord who judges me (P3)".

In true SE you do not need to "judge" others (Lk. 6:37,41). Because you live above the opinions of others, you know that others do not need your opinion. What others think about you will not have any effect on THEIR happiness or destiny. In other words, it's only what they think about Jesus Christ and divine viewpoint that matters NOT what they think about you.

Self-Esteem

In true self-esteem you are not "hurt" by the criticisms of others nor are you "stimulated" by the flattery of others. Why: Because your SE is not dependent on your RELATIONSHIP with them. Your SE is dependent on your relationship with your Father. Only He knows everything about you (Ps. 139) and only He loves you with a love beyond anything known to man (l Jn. 4:10, 3:1; Jn. 15:13; Ps. 32:10).

Your Father is always fair and accurate (Ps. 33:5; Rom. 2:11).

2 Cor. 3:4-6; "Such CONFIDENCE (true SE) as this is ours through Christ before God. Not that we are competent in ourselves (counterfeit SE) but our COMPETENCE comes from God (source of true SE)". Confidence + Competence = true self-esteem . . . Not from people or from self but from RPD.

Jesus said to the religious crowd, "and do not think you can say to yourselves, 'We have Abraham as our father' . . . Matthew 3:9. Point: SE is NOT built on human relationships, even with your ancestors.

SE comes from an abiding persistent loyalty to that which is of the greatest value of all (Matt. 4:4, 24:35).

SE is a confidence and fortitude that gives you strength and poise under pressure. You have a deep satisfaction that you are doing the right thing and you stand for the right thing. You don't NEED flattery, contests, prizes, awards, or other recognition because you are no longer dependent on the opinion of others about you—good or bad. You know WHO you are and WHERE you are going! (Jn. 8:14)

"You are my Son, whom I love; with you I am well pleased" (Lk. 3:22). Just as God the Father said this about Jesus, He can also say it about you . . . it's up to you. Would this not give you all the SE you could ever want?

It's simple. If you NEED the 6A, you NEED people and their acceptance. And if you are not happy without them (6A people), not confident, and not content then you are dependent, fragile, insecure, weak, and uncertain. You have EDS.

Building SE on the winnings of competition with others and the applause of admirers is a TRAP to lead you into a life of contests with people and "comparison living". You are LURED to do all you do for the reward of self-promotion and recognition. This is an arrogance role—not true SE. The religious crowd of Jesus' day were prime examples. He pointed this out to us in Matt. 23:5-7. "Everything they do is done for men to SEE . . . They love the place of honor . . . they love to be greeted . . ."

"To these same people (6A types) Jesus said "How can you believe if you accept praise from one another, yet make no effort to obtain the praise that comes from God" (Jn. 5:44). Jesus spoke this to self-confident people. Their confidence was built on praise (6A) from people—self and others. Notice carefully in this verse that there is an EITHER OR situation, that is, when you are struggling for the 6A of man you are NOT making any "effort" to please God.

P4. While keeping your eyes on people, focusing on what they think about you, it is impossible to live the life of faith. Note: "How can you BELIEVE if you accept praise (6A) from men . . ." (Jn. 5:44). No can do. It is FAITH that pleases God (Heb. 11:6; Lk. 22:32; Ps. 147:11; Lk. 18:8, 8:25).

P5. Tune out what people think about you, FOCUS on what GOD thinks about you and you will have S.E.

True SE does not COMPETE with PEOPLE. It doesn't live in comparison with others in ANY way. In fact, it has absolutely NOTHING to do with others. This is what makes it so satisfying and stable—it is independent of all things that are changeable, weak, and unpredictable. It is only and entirely dependent on the ONLY immutable, powerful, and trustworthy thing in life—GOD. His integrity, His love for you ensures your SE will ALWAYS be intact, enduring, and indestructible (Rom. 2:29).

"For I am convinced that neither death nor life, neither angels or demons, neither the present not the future, nor any powers, neither height nor depth, nor anything else in all creation, will be able to separate us from the LOVE OF GOD that is in Christ Jesus our Lord" (Rom. 8:38-39).

Your faith in God's love for you is the antidote, the vaccine that makes ANY feelings of worthlessness, inferiority, or self-abasement IMPOSSIBLE. You are no longer BELOW anyone just as you are never above anyone (Matt. 23:8-12).

Human love for you is dependent on your having attractive desirable qualities. If you don't have them then you are rejected. This love is always conditional; if you change your face, your body or your behavior you may lose the love you treasure. What does this have to do with self-esteem? Well, that you cannot build self-esteem on being loved or accepted by this kind of love (which is the MAJORITY of love and romance)! A minority of people have enough integrity in their soul so that they do have a higher form of love. They don't require you to be attractive or impressive, they love you because THEY have integrity, that is, they don't have to be PERSONALLY pleased or impressed by your qualities, they love out of their own quality, their integrity.

This is the kind of love that God has. It is this love and only this love on which you can build your own SE. His love for you will NEVER change because it does NOT depend on your thoughts, actions, looks, past, awards, skills, grades, degrees, IQ, success, family, income, possessions, pedigree, health, or arrest record! (Read Lk. 15:11-22).

Emotion

Good emotions should be the product of good thought. All kinds of good emotion will come from right beliefs and good knowledge (like a pear comes from a pear tree). The pear is not the tree, it is the fruit of the tree. The pear doesn't make anything . . . the tree makes the pear, but if it didn't make a pear (emotion) it would still be a pear tree. Some pear trees don't make pears you know, and some do sometimes. Of course, some people are more emotional than others. In fact, this is one reason why emotion itself cannot be the real measure of right and wrong, truth and error, spiritual and secular . . . because it does vary from person to person. We know . . .

P1. Everyone has EQUAL opportunity to be right and spiritual regardless of their ability to emote.

Before you go any further I want to issue you a warning. You who do not want peace of mind and a relaxed mental attitude . . . who prefer to argue, sulk, pout, grieve, brood, whine, worry, be afraid, tense, angry, or hypersensitive should NOT read this essay.

Those who are emotional have more feeling: I want to use this word because it is the one we use and hear most often. We don't usually say I emote . . . we say I feel this or that. Remember good and bad emotion? The word "feeling" will be used for both. Everyone wants to "feel" good . . . both physically and emotionally. To feel good physically a person can "work out" physically. And guess what? To feel good emotionally . . . a person can "work out" emotionally. You see emotional feelings (good and bad) can be a natural product of what you think or believe AND they can be generated by OUTSIDE influence like music, rhythm, passion, entertainment, color, beauty, shock, surprise, and preachers! Now I love good emotion but I, like you, need to be sure that it is NEVER emotion that controls my life. It can NOT be the measure of my happiness. Emotions go up and down. They are fickle and fragile, unreliable, and often entirely independent of what we want to believe in. Don't be an emotional- feelings junkie . . . or you will definitely be disappointed down the road. There is no such thing as "feeling" spiritual . . . there is no Biblical support for such an idea. If you "tingle" when in church some day that's fine, but it's probably because of what's going on around you. I have studied the work of the Holy Spirit in the Bible and nowhere does it reveal that His job is to make you tingle or "feel" anything. You must understand that there is a difference between a physical sensation such as tingling or energy and the mental state of mind of joy and happiness. God gives you happiness through the truth . . . should you believe it. Once you do learn and believe it . . . as a happy person you might then tingle or vibrate. He guarantees the happiness (Jn. 10:10) but NOT the emotional part.

"Feelings" indeed are tricky. Do not focus on your feelings (FOF). If you do you will be distracted from the truth. It is the truth . . . in your mind that gives you contentment, confidence, and stability. If you are always thinking of how you feel emotionally—good or bad - then you are ignoring what you believe or you might begin to . . . then you will sink or rise depending on how you feel at the moment. Remember those outside influences I wrote of earlier . . . they can "sift you like wheat" and make you draw wrong conclusions. Always consult what you KNOW and what you BELIEVE. These are your measures of mental and spiritual well-being.

Many believers have a weakness for the distractions of emotionalism and entertainment. These two distractions (from spiritual reality) include excitement, rhythm, eloquence, personality love, contest, showmanship, and many other "feel good" sensory turn-ons. These distractions are temptations designed to divert your attention away from growing in "grace and knowledge" (2 Pet. 3: 18) through the routine intake of accurately taught Bible doctrine.

I have given you two list now of items that are often sources of emotional stimulation. Note I did NOT say these sources are bad, evil, or useless. On the contrary, some of these sources contain a lot of good . . . but they CAN BE distracting IF you are focusing on the feeling (FOF) they give you. God is seeking worshipers to worship Him in "spirit and truth" (Jn. 4:23-24). He is not interested in your emotional feeling. "Spirit" refers to your soul and also has to do with the invisible yet live aspect of your relationship with Him. Some people have some truth or knowledge about God in their heads, but there is no real spiritual relationship. "Spirit" does not refer to emotion . . . Emotion is human. God is Spirit. God is not emotional . . . humans are. Jesus was emotional . . . as a human. Please don't confuse being spiritual with being emotional, healthy, or having a great personality, or being active. I believe Jesus Christ had all of these traits and He always had GOOD emotion . . . but it was not these traits that were the reason for His spirituality. He was the epitome of spiritual life because He was the WORD (Jn. 1:1), He was the TRUTH (Jn. 14:6), and He was the LIGHT (Jn. 8:12). These words are all synonyms for KNOWLEDGE.

In 1 Peter 1, Peter repeatedly emphasizes knowledge as the NECESSARY element for spiritual standing four times in the first eight verses.

In Ephesians 1, Paul states in his prayer for them that they "may KNOW Him better" (v17). Then that they "may KNOW the hope" to which they are called (v18). (See also Phil. 1:9 and Col. 1:10).

The word emotion or feel is almost never used in Scripture. What does that tell you? The words knowledge, truth, and faith are used greatly. This is because emotion is a human product of thinking the truth. The best emotion will come out when the truth is put into your heart, mind, and soul. When you bear the fruit of the Spirit, . . . which are love, joy, etc. (Gal. 5:22), these are not emotions . . . they are what the Bible says they are, that is, "fruits of the Spirit." Emotions are human . . . fruits of the Spirit are divine. So here is the principle:

P2. To teach or promote emotion is NOT found in the Bible.

P3. There are repeated mandates in the Bible to teach and learn spiritual truth.

The best Scriptural example I can give you is the entire letter of 1 John. The human quality of feeling is so prevalent and overrated that it is common to hear people say, "I feel this or that to be true, etc." Now look at what is in John's letter TO YOU. He uses the words "know, know the truth, light, word, faith, teach, believe" . . . see refs: 1:1,5-8, 2:3-5, 8-10, 13-14, 18, 20-21,29, 3:1-2, 5-6, 10, 14, 16, 18-19, 23-24, 4:1, 6-8, 13, 16, 5:1-2, 4-6, 10, 13, 15, 18-20.

In almost all verses there is the emphasis of knowledge. In many of them it is found twice. The word used the great majority of the time is KNOW!

Suppose John was the FEELING type instead of the KNOWING type. Then some of the verses might read like this: "I write these things to you who believe in the name of the Son of God so that you may FEEL (rather than know) you have eternal life" (5:13) OR "And if we FEEL (rather than know) that He hears us—whatever we ask—we FEEL (rather than know) that we have what we asked of Him (5:15). MORE. "We FEEL also that the Son of God has come . . . " (v20). Try this yourself by substituting the word "feel" into the verses I gave you earlier in 1 John. "Feel" often fits quite easily into such other verses as 2:3, 29, 3:3, 5, 14, 19, 4:13, 5:1-2, 5. Note particularly 3:24, ". . . and this is how we FEEL that He lives in us: We FEEL it by the Spirit He gave us." NO, NOT, NEVER! We KNOW by the Spirit. The Spirit gives knowledge . . . NOT feeling! This verse is explicit. Summary point:

    P4.   What you KNOW about God and His plan is everything . . . what you FEEL about it is not an issue . . . not vital.

Emotion is not primary, it is secondary. Good emotion results from APPRECIATION for the truth (doctrine) you believe. Good emotion is a responder. It is not the focus or the criteria for anything, it is only the result. When the truth is the focus and the priority in your life, then your emotion will be appropriate, positive, and rewarding. THEN you will also have the proper values for the items I listed as SOURCES of emotion. They won't be over-rated and over-indulged . . . at the expense of growing in knowledge . . . learning.

Did you know that evil people feel good when their evil plans succeed? IS that a stupid question? Of course. This means that emotion doesn't know right from wrong. You might even feel good over something or some belief that is totally wrong! Does this surprise you? Increase your knowledge of Bible truth and decrease your surprises.

Symptoms and signs of emotional distraction and FOF are common. Most common is ups and downs in your spiritual life . . . poor motivation . . . seeking out stimulating services or programs to get you going or "revive" you.

Many people often seek help to get free of bad emotion because it usually also feels bad . . . such as fear, worry, or anger. (Tit 3:3 refers to people "enslaved and deceived" by bad emotion). Once you have allowed emotion to rule your soul it is difficult to take control again. How did this happen? If your mind is not filled with truth from which it can direct your life, your decisions, and your emotions or if you reject the truth that you hear . . . emotion takes over. Your frame of reference (FOR) becomes your emotion (good and bad). Emotion doesn't know right from wrong, so you have no stability, no confidence . . . and as time goes by, the negative emotions DOMINATE the positive emotions . . . fear beats up on faith, anger blocks out forgiveness, and etc. Of course, this extreme doesn't develop in everyone . . . it only develops to the extent that anyone rejects the truth . . . or as Jesus described it, "walks in darkness" (Jn. 12:35).

The solution to control of your soul, spiritual stability and advancement begins with stopping your FOF and getting a new FOR. This is done by focusing on doctrine (FOD). SUBSTITUTION is the dynamic principle you should be aware of. It is going on all the time. If and when you say no to the truth you will get a substitute. With emotion in control, you have a substitute FOR. What do you do to get rid of a substitute? Right . . . you substitute!

Faith and truth must substitute for fear and feelings. Your new focus will take a lot of time in emotional rehabilitation. While routine spiritual growth requires a lot of time taking in the Word of God, emotional rehabilitation requires INTENSE intake of Bible doctrine. What do I mean by intense? One or two hours per day minimum. Unfortunately, most pastors and church ministries do not provide this intensity of teaching on a continuous basis (and it does need to be continuous). But if you are positive, hungry, motivated, and most of all HUMBLE, that is, teachable, then you are ready to advance out of a life of emotional instability into maturity which includes calm, peace, and poise, with a relaxed mental attitude. As a teachable believer you are ready to advance

Emotion 61

on at all costs. You are more willing to lay aside ANY non-Biblical non-issue items in your way. These MAY include family beliefs, tradition, denomination ties, emotional stimulants (see prior lists) or personal attachments to family, friends, or social circles (church, clubs, etc.) that are distracting you from study, learning, and time to do so. You don't need me or anyone else to tell you where to go, who to listen to, or what to read. If you place yourself in the open teachable frame of mind, then you are automatically taken care of by God Himself under the promise and doctrine of "Full Disclosure" (see essay). Simply stated, the central principle of this doctrine says that God will see to it that you have full disclosure (accurate understanding) of ALL the doctrine and divine viewpoint which you are WILLING to BELIEVE.

Bible teaching on this matter is large. A few references are: ". . . Seek and you will find . . . he who seeks finds" (Matt. 7:7). Be a finder! "THEN you will know the truth and the truth will set you FREE" (Jn. 8:31). Free from emotional bondage. "But when He, the Spirit of TRUTH, comes, He will guide you into ALL truth" (Jn. 16:13). Equal opportunity. ". . . ANYONE who comes to Him (God) must believe that He exists and that He rewards those who earnestly seek Him" (Heb. 11:6). Synthesis goes like this:

P5. The finder is freed, guided, and rewarded! For further progress and maintenance up the hill to "higher ground" remember:

P6. How you feel emotionally OR physically has nothing to do with your spiritual status or progress.

Never does God promise the advancing believer a feel good experience. She may feel good and energetic with joy and singing, etc., or he may feel down due to poor energy or disease. Do not let feelings be a CONFUSION factor for you. If you do then you become vulnerable to false doctrine, deception, non-issues, and counterfeit experiences. You are bait, ripe for the picking, a sucker and a loser. Stay with doctrine, keep on learning and listening to what you read in Scripture, pray for understanding and the truth will set you free . . . free to live the "full life". This God does guarantee (Jn. 10:10)!

"Be joyful always" (I Thes. 5:16).

"give thanks in all circumstances (good and bad)" (v18).

This means that bad emotion is unauthorized. He doesn't want you to have any bad emotion. He has provided a life of faith so you don't need to. At the same time, if you do get bad emotion . . . "He is the Father of compassion and the God of all comfort" for you (2 Cor. 1:3-7). And again, "Now may the Lord of peace Himself give you peace at ALL TIMES and in every way" (2 Thes. 3: 16).

P7. The life of FAITH is one of emotional health and stability under all circumstances.

But remember that this FAITH has to be built up through knowledge of His truth . . . the faith. Your faith (noun) is the Word of God. You can only exercise faith (verb) by knowing the Word of God. Paul was constantly telling Timothy this, " . . . in the truths of the faith and the good teaching that you have followed" (1 Tim. 4:6), "devote yourself to them . . ." (v16). "Study to show yourself approved a workman . . ." (II Tim. 2:15, 3:16-17; Heb. 4:12).

P8. The more of THE faith you know, the more faith you can exercise.

There is only ONE humanly possible action that was ever said to amaze or impress Jesus while He was here. It was FAITH! See Lk. 7:9, Matt. 15:38, and Heb. 11:6, " . . . and without FAITH it is impossible to please God."

Emotion

P9. While good emotion is a product of faith in the truth, bad emotion is a product of shallow or no faith (Lk. 8:24-25; Jn. 14:1,27).

If you gave the truth to someone and they were positive about it . . . they received it with a lot of positive VISIBLE emotion and excitement, what would you think? You would be led to think the best about that person by what you see and the more emotion he or she puts out the more you would be impressed with their reception of the truth. Perhaps. Look at Matt. 13:20-21:

"The one who received the seed that fell on rocky places is the man who hears the word (truth) and at once receives it with JOY. But since he has no ROOT, he lasts only a short time. When trouble or persecution comes because of the word, he quickly falls away."

P10. Spiritually speaking, you can't tell anything about anyone by observing their emotions.

One of the most outstanding factors about the spiritual life ... the life of faith is that it is INVISIBLE. You might also ask what is "root" (v21)? I believe root is FAITH. "Root" is . . . guess what . . . invisible . . . not felt, not seen, not heard. 2 Cor. 5:7 says, "We live by faith, NOT by sight."

P11. Don't be an artificial plant, get all the "ROOT" you can and grow (Matt. 13 :20-21; 2 Pet. 3: 18; Col. 1:10).

BACK TO BASICS

Emotion comes from the soul and it is FELT in the body and EXPRESSED through the body. (By the way, this is one reason we know God does not have emotion. He is a spirit. .. He doesn't have a body or soul). Now if you have given emotion control of your soul, it will grow strong and have a greater effect on your body.

The super-emotion person I like to call HYSTERIC, which I define as jerky, flighty, jumpy, easily distracted, impatient, tense, and often has "oral urgency" . . . another term of mine which describes those who can't wait to talk. Of course, not everyone becomes this symptomatic. Here's a test for you. In a human conflict someone's feelings are hurt. Do you think the person with the hurt feelings is the one deserving satisfaction, because he is hurt? If so, then you are FOF. You think feelings the FOR for what is right. NOT! Feelings are not like a wind vane . . . always pointing in the right direction. This is especially true about "hurt". The people who "hurt" the most are those who are most sensitive or vulnerable . . . that is, those who are most emotional.

Okay, none of the above describes you. I'm glad. Here is you . . . It is enough, yeah, more than enough to know that God has me by my right hand (Ps. 16 and 73), knows me (Ps. 139), and is in me (Jn. 14:20). I do not NEED feelings—good or bad emotion—to have this confidence. In fact I do not want feelings to support these facts. Because feelings are human and unreliable.

The word of God says these things to me therefore I KNOW them to be true. This is faith. Music, eloquence, or people can not make them any more true than they already are. The strength of my faith is in my knowledge and belief of His word.

I FEEL the need to repeat myself some . . . You can get good feelings from having a strong belief in something. Even if what you believe is wrong this can happen . . . because you are convinced you are right. Feelings of loyalty, sacrifice, achievement, and compassion can all flow from your mistaken belief . . . making all these "positive" feelings in fact negative. How? They are positive only from human viewpoint. Divine viewpoint is concerned only with the truth . . . not the feeling. See how fickle feelings are? Now you FOF people need to hear this. People can't even tell whether a feeling is good or bad by how it feels! That's because feelings have no way of KNOWING what the truth is. They only respond to what you THINK. If you think something is true and really love it . . . you will feel all positive inside . . . whether it is true or not! Therefore, feelings are NEVER indications of right or wrong, truth or error.

Believers are told in Romans 12 to mourn with those who mourn. This is showing concern for their misery. Jesus did this, once for the misery of mourners in John 11 and once for those who would mourn later under discipline, i.e., Jerusalem (Lk. 13:34-35, 19:41). In both cases He wept. But not because these people were feeling bad. He was distressed because of the REASON they were feeling bad or in Jerusalem's case, would feel bad. The reason for their misery and discipline was lack of faith. Misery was the symptom . . . lack of faith (unbelief) was the disease.

P12. The only time God is honored by a sadness on your part, or even anger, is when you are responding to something that dishonors Him (Mk. 3:5).

Here I go again: Good emotion follows good thought. Good emotion is determined by what you think . . . not by what you feel. Jesus wept. Was that good emotion? YES. Why? Because He was thinking the right things . . . good things . . . divine viewpoint. Did it "feel" good? Probably not . . . what determines if an emotion is good or bad. Not the f___g but the t____t. This is why we have to learn what to think . . . get a right FOR. This is why it is dangerous to FOF.

"Set your minds (FOR) on things above NOT on earthly (human) things (FOF)" (Col. 3:1-2).

God is always the first object of your concern. If you focus on and accept what God thinks about any event or situation in life—whether good or bad from the human viewpoint—you will always think the right thing which will produce positive emotion.

The best emotion is positive. Positive emotion responds to awareness of God and truth. The more aware you become the greater your emotion . . . more intense and satisfying. The more you learn about God, the more truth you learn, the greater your potential for positive emotional experiences. I say "potential" to remind you that some are more or less emotional depending on their biology and personality.

Reasons for this essay:

1. Stamp out confusion about emotion and spirituality.

2. Explain good and bad emotion.

3. Show that emotion is not a measure of spirituality OR an indicator of truth.

4. Emotion (good or bad) does not sanction the truth . . . but TRUTH sanctions emotion.

5. To promote faith and truth as the way to a peaceful, stable emotional life.

Some ask, "Suppose some person doesn't believe in God, or Jesus, or the Bible? How can this information help that person?"

In my physician role, sometimes a patient has a condition for which there is only ONE medicine. Believe it or not, no one (in my experience of approximately 200,000 patient encounters) has ever cared about that . . . as long as that medicine works!

Sympathy

When you see someone hurting emotionally, whether due to loss, abuse, or their own negative behavior, you naturally want to help them . . . or show sympathy somehow. That is, assuming you are an "average" human being. As you know, some of us are more human than others and some are "less than average"! I have already mentioned to you before under the good and bad principle that there is good and bad sympathy. That leads to why I am writing this . . . it is because I want people who need sympathy to get good sympathy so they will be helped, and so God will be honored by the behavior of those who are hurting. Are you surprised? Even in the time of hurt; in fact, especially in the time of hurt, it still is God who is of first concern . . . what does He think, what does He "feel", what does He expect? This is most important.

If you are not aware of this or don't believe it, then you are not qualified to be a sympathizer. You can, of course, still give sympathy and FEEL VERY sympathetic but you are giving low quality sympathy or "bad" sympathy. Good sympathy provides solutions, real support, help, objectivity . . . listening to the point of understanding. Good sympathy realizes the hurt person is being tested and probably needs to be reminded of this fact. Now its true that FEW people want to hear that the problems of life are tests, and few want to hear the solution . . . especially if they are in negative emotion all the time. But remember, there are also FEW who are "chosen" and FEW who find the narrow road that leads to life (Matt. 7:14).

People who settle for low-quality sympathy, who just want attention and "emotional support" are gratified to an extent, appreciative, and consoled. But when this small measure of "success" is DEPENDENT on the stroking, understanding, and attention you gave them, guess what? . . . They will need more of it . . . perhaps over and over for a long time. Hence we have another form of attention deficit disorder, ADD! Is this you, someone you know, or both?

The worst part about the person who rejects their tests AND the solution to their test is twofold:

1. You good sympathizers out there have your hands tied. You can try to express love to them with spiritual support and encouragement but your ministry and therefore the plan of God is blocked by negative emotion and negative volition.

2. God is not honored. Every test that "hurts" a person is intended by God to direct their attention to Him (Amos 4:6-11; 1 Pet. 1:6-7; Js. 1:2-4,12). He is, and offers the solution to hurt, pain, loss, abuse, or adversity. Faith honors Him AND relieves the pain.

Self-pity is promoted by poor sympathy. The classic Biblical example of this is the Book of Job. When Job's three friends ". . . heard about all his trouble . . . they set out to go and sympathize with him and comfort him" (2:11). Job's sympathizers misled him . . . Job fell into self-pity (7:11-21), but recovered when he acknowledged God's sovereignty (authority) (40-41, especially verses 1-2,6-7; 41:11, and 42:1-6). Verse 6 says that Job despised himself and repented! This is a man who had incredible loss, tragedy, and yes . . . HURT! Why did he need to repent? He fell into self-pity with the help of low-quality SYMPATHY. This mental attitude sin is self-centered . . . it is arrogance! You see the arrogant are not the snobs . . . they are the miserable. Why? Because they reject

Sympathy 69

God's comfort, His faith solution, His purpose for this testing. An important principle about life is this: The solution to life's problems and the purpose of life are one!

It is fascinating to me that probably the oldest, first written account of human behavior was Job . . . an account of personal trial and tragedy. Notice please how intimately God is involved in this account . . . from the authorization of the tragedy, through Job's positive AND negative reactions to it, and then the positive ending resulting from Job's positive response of confession and faith.

Listen to Job's own estimation of his sympathizers (counselors): " . . . have proved to be of no help" (6:21). " . . . you are worthless physicians, all of you. If only you would be altogether SILENT" (13:4). " . . . miserable comforters all of you" (16:2).

You may recall that initially Job would not cave in to self-pity. His wife advised him to do so! He said no to her! (Brave man.) But where his wife (unsympathetic) had failed, his friends (sympathetic, 2:11) succeeded. She was direct, abrupt, harsh, and negative. Job could see her mental attitude sin easily. Not so with his friendly sympathizers. They were subtle, relentless, caring, and emotional (2: 12-13). This was hard to resist and over time, bad sympathy broke Job's integrity . . . he started to focus on himself just as he was encouraged to do. After seven days of their "therapy", Job broke . . . and said "3:1-ff".

In what way did Job "give up his integrity"? (To get in on the principle with which I am about to shock you, you should at least read Job 1:6-2:11, and at the very least Job 2:3-11.) Job lost his integrity when he went FROM 2:10 accepting good and bad from God without any VERBAL sin (blame, complain, ask why, etc.), TO 3:1 . . . verbal sinning (complaining, whining, and bemoaning throughout much of the rest of the book). Now here is the shocker.

P1. When a person suffers loss, is in pain and hurt, and responds with complaining, self-pity, or goes on a sympathy search or a blaming spree . . . this person has NO integrity.

You can be an accomplice to sin as well as you can to crime. Aiding and abetting the faithless is dangerous ground. Being sympathetic to the complaining is NOT a virtue. Don't get lost in your feelings for the "victims". Don't support behavior in others which is insulting to God. Try to accept the fact that there are people who prefer sorrow to faith and tears to joy. They will NEVER accept the fact that God loves them and will manage and protect their lives . . . In addition, heaven is not the preferred environment of these people (Rev. 21:4).

Listen to the world's all time good sympathizer. In Luke 10, Martha is seen "worried and upset" (v41). She was "distracted" by many details (v40). In this state of misery, she accused the Lord of not caring (v40)! Guess what? He told her to RE-FOCUS . . . off the details and onto the ONE necessary thing . . . the truth (v42) (Lk. 10:27-28; Matt. 4:4)! Jesus did NOT acknowledge her feelings verbally. Martha misjudged Jesus' concern for her:

P2. Relaxed people . . . because they have their priorities right . . . will be accused by those in "imaginary living" of being unaware and insensitive.

Then again in John 11, Martha was mourning the loss of her brother when she said to Jesus, "Lord, if you had been here, my brother would not have died . . ." (v21). I'm not implying anything negative about Martha here . . . just notice how once again Jesus does NOT acknowledge her feelings verbally but goes directly to challenging her faith by saying, "Your brother will rise again" (v23). Caring, informing, and focusing on who?

For two more examples of the Lord's response in situations which call for sympathy see Lk. 8:22-25 and Lk. 13:1-5.

Sympathy

You, as a good sympathizer, must develop your own speech to help people in pain. In doing so, think of where God fits into what is going on. Don't focus on feelings or say things that encourage the hurt person to focus on their feelings. Can you imagine me telling a patient, "Now I want you to focus on your pain?" NO. Don't discourage good emotion, in fact, join in . . . cry, weep, and mourn (Rom. 12:15). If the hurt is new or recent . . . then this may not be the time for talk . . . emotional times are not good times for learning or teaching. You might only say, "I'm sorry for your loss, or . . . is there anything I can do?" This may open up the door for a later opportunity to ask if they understand why God allowed this loss in their life. A favorite of mine to say to someone left behind after the death of a loved one is, "If he was a believer, then I'm sure he is NOT disappointed." This focuses their situation outside themselves, on something positive, and it has always been met with positive responses. I like what Dr. Warren Wiersbe, noted pastor, author, and Bible expositor says in his Vol. 1, New Testament, p. 352 . . . "We usually think of 'comfort' as soothing someone, consoling him or her; and to some extent this is true. But true comfort strengthens us to face life bravely and keep on going. It does not rob us of responsibility or make it easy for us to give up."

Here is a personal family story to help illustrate a point. My stepmother, who raised me, and I, took my father to a distant site for alcohol rehab. Upon attempting to leave, he began to cry and threaten to harm himself if we left him alone. Because of pity for him my stepmother would not make him stay in spite of the fact that we all knew he desperately needed help . . . he was already killing himself. Of course she loved him . . . but emotional pity is no substitute for real compassion. How do you tell the difference? Simply do the best and right thing for the benefit of the one you are concerned about. They may not even want it or know it. Pity rescues others from their personal stress, while love helps them to make life adjustments to prevent damage. Guilt is another indicator. To be brief, if you do what is best for someone and you feel guilty about it, what is the problem? It's all about focus.

Often, especially toward someone who is negatively charged, it is better for them for you to stand back and let them experience the negative consequences of their actions. This is the "reap what you sow" principle (Gal. 6:7). It's God's way of teaching responsibility, accountability, and justice. We say "live and learn." Don't interfere with this process because you pity them. They need to learn. Don't self-indulge your emotions at their expense.

Jesus loved Jerusalem (Lk. 19:41-44). He wept over their rejection of the truth. He did not rescue them. He offered them the solution and warned them. He pronounced severe discipline on them to come.

> P3. Love and compassion is never opposed to discipline or justice. Discipline and justice are good . . . not bad.

We are authorized, encouraged, and commanded to have compassion for others. In this way, we express the grace and integrity of God as His ambassadors and witnesses. We are NOT authorized to express His justice, in fact, we are forbidden to do so. (Rom. 12:19, " . . . but leave room for God's wrath.")

"Finally, all of you, live in harmony with one another: be SYMPATHETIC, love as brothers, be COMPASSIONATE and humble." (1 Pet. 3:8).

Denial, Defense, and Deception

It is a fact about human nature that all of us have the need and motivation to be approved, innocent, and justified. Generally, you don't even think about this from day to day, but if you are blamed, accused, or disapproved by anyone, an alarm goes off to alert you that your state of serenity and innocence has been threatened! Most of you would become highly motivated at that point to squash any notion that you are at fault, in error, guilty, or otherwise worthy of any disapproval.

Lest I am less than thorough in my description of this natural state of mankind, let me say that people also generally not only resist being blamed or disapproved, they also resist being told they are wrong, and resist being corrected.

Exceptions Wanted

Now I realize that not all people resist blame, correction, or accusation. This is because these people are secure. They have a developed personal integrity which protects them. These people are open and receptive to criticism or correction because they love the truth more than their image. They love honesty and humility more than what people think about them. They want to be corrected because this would improve their lives. They want to change their beliefs and loyalties to a more accurate position because they love absolute truth and want to obey it. They are in a position of strength.

Define Denial

Of course, there is good denial and bad denial (see *Good*

and Bad Principle). Easily, you can see that denial is the proper position for you to take when you know you are innocent OR that you really are correct. This is good denial, and good denial will lead you to good defense. Good defense will act with honesty and integrity to defend yourself ONLY when you are not at fault.

To deny you are at fault or in error when you know you are is bad denial. Denial is everywhere. Criminals get up in court and deny their crime. Children, full of themselves, deny disobedience. Teenagers often deny they have poor values. Adults deny they are hypocrites, even though they demand behavior from others that they themselves do not produce.

'Active' denial is "when someone or your conscience accuses or corrects you and you REJECT the truth. 'Passive' denial is when you declare you believe something (like religion) but you know you really do not believe it or live it. When you deny a double life, a double standard (a position of weakness), or when you deny addiction, or simply continue to refuse to confess personal sins, then you are "living in denial". Living in denial means you REFUSE to accept truth about something, you refuse to take responsibility for your action, you refuse to examine your beliefs and practices to improve them, or you refuse to be proactive to SEEK a greater integrity than you have.

Degrees of Denial

My friends, if you are complacent about where you are in life. If you are content to NOT weed out the garden of your life or clean out the corners of your mind, then you are apathetic. This IS living in denial. Why? Because you are DENYING that you need to do these things, the things you need to do to improve your integrity, your knowledge, and your love for your CREATOR.

Living in denial is stressful, counterproductive, and SAD (see glossary). This stress is good AND bad. It is bad because it has a bad origin. It is good because you are reaping what you

Denial, Defense, and Deception 75

sowed. Your Creator instituted reaping what you sow for your benefit. When you sow a life of denial, through self-indulgence or apathy, you will reap fear of loss, insecurity, weakness, boredom, and frustration. Those negative consequences are part of another principle your Creator has graciously provided you. I call it the Push-Pull Principle (PPP).

The PPP goes like this. When God's integrity appeals to you and you pursue that integrity, then this is His pull on you. You are "pulled" to Him by His attraction to you. When integrity is not a higher priority in your life and you feel the PAIN of denial then this pain should "push" you to turn around and pursue the course He created for you; absolute honesty and absolute truth (a short definition of Integrity).

Believe me, if you are in a life of frustration, discouragement, disillusionment, disappointment, or boredom then you ARE living in denial. If you are here and don't want to CHANGE then you will seek human solutions . . . quick, easy, and sometimes pleasing distractions to comfort yourself or take the "pressure" off. Perhaps good things you can do to impress or appeal to those who may be your accusers, or your victims. Many people spend their whole life doing this. It is a charade, a pretend, and a weak position vulnerable to loss or even the threat of loss. You are pretending everything is OKAY even though you know you are not forgiving someone, or that you are holding on to a religious belief that says others not in your church are not going to heaven! You are also convincing those around you everything is OKAY because you are having fun and they see that. You are in a large group of people who are doing and believing the same as you do and they see that. Now you are feeling better because you are OKAY with yourself (for now) and others are OKAY with you. Group approval, family, or religious approval for you is a potent medicine for the disease of denial. Problem is, this is not a cure. It is only what we call a defense mechanism; remember this term, and more about it later.

I am writing about denial because it is so devastating, destructive, self-defeating, and self-serving. It destroys integrity, prevents integrity, destroys relationships, and creates so much collected grief, conflict, stress, lying, loneliness, anger, and many others. Denial is the exact opposite of confession. It is the opposite of love for the truth. It means to dispute, renounce, disown, and hate the truth. When in our court system the accused stands and takes the position of "not guilty," this is often the beginning of public denial-which is unfortunately supported by legal procedure. Denial leads to and in fact, demands DEFENSE. This is true in court and true in life.

Why do so many so often choose to deny the truth about themselves or about those they may be defending? Several reasons come to mind but the most basic and fundamental of all is the all time ever present great-FEAR OF LOSS. Telling the truth about yourself or someone else may be accompanied by loss, loss of face, loss of reputation, loss of status, job, security, property, relationship, comfort, peace, good opinion from others, income, or your own personal pet possession.

Remember I am referring to "bad" denial, that denial which is dishonest and self-serving. Good denial is when you deny what you know you are truly innocent of. Innocence has no guilt. Guilt is a product of "bad" denial. The solution to guilt is confession. The prevention of guilt is a right value system and a love for integrity, God, and others.

While denial is used by many as a solution to escape loss and the fear of loss (FOL), it is NOT a good choice. It is a quick fix, human solution which indeed may PREVENT the loss you fear but will PRODUCE a new set of problems for you: 1. Guilt, 2. The need to Justify your position, which can be an ongoing effort, 3. Low self-esteem, 4. Low integrity, 5. Possibly severed relationship-between you and God as well as you and others, perhaps even someone close to you!

Denial, Defense, and Deception 77

So you see, even the human solution to your sin or misbehavior- your denial of error-DOES cost you. You may not lose what you fear losing, like your innocence, but you will lose things listed above and you will lose the benefit of the most important relationship you were created for. God does not tolerate denial. In no way is He pleased with you if you determine to live in denial of any bad or bogus behavior OR belief!

In the courtroom of your conscience, you are not to deny the truth and become your own defense attorney. This is rebellion against God's procedure. It is a violation of the method He has provided for you to keep yourself free of court time. Stay out of court, confess your sin, and forgive your neighbor. This is normal, natural, and physically, mentally, and spiritually healthy. If you refuse to practice confession and forgiveness then you will naturally move into the defense of your position- "not guilty".

True Denial

Denial is rejection of the truth . . . truth about God, about reality, about life, responsibility you have, or truth about yourself or others. A rejecter in denial of any of these things IS living in denial. Persistence in denial motivates you to take a stand, a position which will justify your choice. Self-justification is what you do when you defend your position. You need self-justification to get rid of guilt, maintain your attitude, feel better, and walk away from honesty and humility!

This denial may be denial of the truth about how you have mistreated someone, been unfair, or exaggerated your status. It may be denying that you have minimized or rejected someone else's belief when in fact you have not even thought about their belief. You could be in denial that you are not giving as much as you should, or that you are not forgiving all that you should. You may be in denial that you are critical of people who don't live like you do. Perhaps you deny that you hold on to beliefs, doctrines, or a church that you really don't agree with. Perhaps you are not taking a stand for what you know is true and honest. You deny God loves you when you fear. You deny God's word when you look outside of it for life. You deny God your life when you demand to control your own destiny. You deny Christ to be your Lord when you pursue what the world loves rather that what He loves.

These, my friend, are examples of a life of DENIAL. It is a life of weakness. You may not feel weak but you will when threats of loss come and when people challenge your self-satisfaction, or when others mistreat you. This is often called STRESS by a large number of people. This is a word you choose which makes you seem more like a victim, and therefore somehow excuses you to feel the way you do. This is not to say stress is always self-inflicted. Often it is, but I mean to say that external stress-from outside sources-are overcoming you BECAUSE you do not have the integrity to protect you from it IF you are in denial-a position of weakness (see *Pursuit of Integrity*).

Do you believe God is a real person who is your Creator? If you answer 'yes' then my next question to you is this. Do you believe you have any real obligation to God? If you do, then you can not possibly live in denial of that obligation; not happily, not stress free, and not in a position of strength. You cannot refuse to do what you should. Reality is that you are to be responsible in your obligation to your Creator, to submit to His will, to love, confess, obey, forgive, and to stop ALL denial and self-justification.

Denial Demands Defense

Have you ever met someone who is never wrong? I have, and I can tell you they are unhappy people. They can become lonely and needy. They have conflict in their lives because never being wrong is not appreciated by those around them-those who are wrong. When you deny your error, sin, mistake, weakness, flaws, or bad choices then you are now pursuing self-justification. That is, denial of a truth about yourself or others motivates you to

Denial, Defense, and Deception

JUSTIFY your denial. Otherwise, you will suffer guilt or some mental anguish knowing that you are not taking responsibility for your error in behavior OR belief. Self-justification is a human solution that avoids confession, avoids responsibility, avoids love for the truth, and avoids embarrassment or possible ridicule. You feel there is a risk of loss of your personal value system so you do not confess anything that might reduce your position in the eyes of others. Instead you use a human solution-you self justify-you justify yourself.

Now there are many ways people do this. Some may say, "The devil made me do it." But notice that even in this denial there is a semi-confession. You are saying that you did it! Watch out, you might get the blame! Do you hate blame? We have an exact word for the attitude of hating the truth about your sin-or any negative thing in your belief and behavior. This word is arrogance. Arrogance hates blame and it hates confession. It pursues NO confession. Those people mentioned earlier who are practically never wrong are suffering from the disease of arrogance. So they seek a DEFENSE to justify their behavior or belief.

There are many ways we proclaim our innocence. This applies to minor things, mind you, as well as to major behaviors or beliefs. For example, it might be something as simple as, "you left the door open, or you forgot to feed the dog, or you didn't tell me." Major violations are, of course, well known to all of us, including disobedience, betrayal, unfaithfulness, laziness, apathy, or excess. When confronted with any of these, today's self-justification MAY sound like one of these statements; "I'm not stupid." "Just kidding." "You think you can do better?" "We can't all be perfect." "You don't know how hard it is." "You don't understand me." "It's much more complex than that." "We've always done it." "What is the truth?" "That's only your opinion." "If only you were in my shoes." "I needed the money." "Everyone else does it." "I'm hurt." "I forgot." "It's always me." "I'm doing the best I can." "No one will ever know."

Well, not only does two wrongs not make a right, but two wrongs also do not make a defense. When you use any such statements as these (or your own personal favorite), you're revealing something about yourself. If you are using these to avoid responsibility for your behavior or belief, then you are telling the world verbally that your integrity is weak. You are proclaiming you are justified when you are not-this is arrogance and hypocrisy.

DEFENSE MECHANISMS

There are many methods people use to defend themselves. These are called "defense mechanisms" (DM). I have a list of about 20 of these! It is no wonder that humans over the course of time could become very creative in the art of self-defense. Today, if you can't defend yourself, you can summon friends to help you (see Sympathy), or you can hire a professional, a defense lawyer, or a counselor.

I will give you a few of the most commonly used defense mechanisms (DM). First is 'projection'. You project your own error onto someone else. For example, when confronted by God, Adam, your father, blamed Eve then Eve blamed the serpent. Projection is blaming another or blaming circumstance that compelled you to misbehave or believe a lie. You might say, "It wasn't me," or, "I couldn't help it," or, "I was misinformed."

Usually it is not God who confronts you. It may be your parents, friends, employer, children, conscience, or even this paper! Projection is blaming, imputing, passing the buck, pointing the finger, and worse, it invites double the guilt now because you are not only rejecting personal responsibility but you are falsely accusing another. Remember, two wrongs do not make a defense. Two wrongs make a pattern; a pattern will lead to more verbal sinning-blaming, criticizing, maligning, and even lying.

Now remember, self-defense is bad only when you are in denial. Denial always leads to self-defense and self-justification. This is because in persistent denial in any area of your life—what

Denial, Defense, and Deception 81

you do or believe—you will find a defense mechanism—a weak human solution.

Another DM is 'compensation'. Rather than confess your error you attempt to make up for it by being nice, humble, caring, or saying things people like to hear. You may do good works, perhaps even some that are directly related to the error you made, or the good you failed to do. God does not accept compensation. He accepts confession only. He tells you in 1 Jn. 1:9 that, "if you will confess your sin, He is faithful and just to forgive your sin and cleanse you from all unrighteousness." This is a good deal-much better than compensation!

Rationalization is a long word but is only a DM that abuses the function of your intelligence (1). You use your God given ability of reason to form an excuse for your failure. For example, you may reason, if this church was good enough for my parents it is good enough for me (regardless of what it teaches). Are you surprised that I use church (or beliefs) in this context about bad behavior? Don't be, because this is a big problem in the area of denial. Believers and unbelievers alike live in a state of denial while sources outside themselves, as well as their conscience, continue to appeal to them they need to examine what they believe in and associate with. Doing nothing is denial. Denial is apathy; it hides, avoids, ignores, rejects, substitutes, and pretends rather than pursue integrity.

Satan's favorite DM is 'identification.' Notice, for fun, that this word has four I's in it! And, in fact, it is all about I. By the way, Satan is in denial, in fact he started it and you join in on his side when you do the same. He points his finger and says to God, "Look they are all doing the same thing I did!" Remember the excuse, "Everybody does it." Now guess where that idea came from? Satan identifies with all those who rebel against the truth. You might identify with these same people by using this DM-identification-to justify yourself. You believe there is comfort in numbers, that is, the majority must be right or "certainly ALL those people-so many for so long-could not possibly be wrong."

This DM is strengthened by popular and powerful personalities to which many weak people gravitate. In their mind they think the impressive personality justifies and validates their liberty to be like, act like, or believe like that person. This reflects the inverted value system of the self-justifier. Poor values lead to poor judgment and poor choices.

'Disassociation' is a bit complex but is a very common DM. It is a double minded life. Therefore it is hypocrisy, yet it is so wide-scale in its practice that it is winked at and used widely to justify much that is bad. For example, many people have a religious life and a secular life, They might say when confronted with an ethical problem, "It's just business," OR, "Yeah, but that is religion." This is also what we call a double-standard. Double standards are everywhere—one standard for religious life and another for routine life. One for you and another for your spouse or neighbor. You disassociate these two opposing and contradictory standards of behavior and belief in your mind. Disassociation means you (humans) have the ability to think about each standard at a time but not think about the contradiction of the two standards in your life. You disconnect one set of rules and beliefs from another set you have then use the one you like when it suits you. For example, your church may teach anyone going to heaven must be a member of it, but you really do not believe that extreme, so you use this DM and live in denial.

'Leveling' or 'Reaction' is a DM developed and used often by more emotional and aggressive people. If you are one of those people, when you become aware of some truth about yourself that you don't like then you will find fault with the source of information, usually a person. You may hear (or say) something as simple as, "Well look who's talking," or, "You can never believe anything he says anyway." The religious people of Jesus' day were

Denial, Defense, and Deception

good at this DM. They would accuse Him, malign Him, or just lie about Him to destroy His credibility, and therefore His message about them. In other words, put simply, you react to the message by attacking the messenger. You bring the source of truth down to a level through fault-finding or vituperation-hence 'leveling.' Lk. 7:33-34 is a good example.

Next is what I call 'fantasy.' Here is where you use your imagination to relieve yourself of responsibility. God gave all of us an imagination. With this function you can create things and ideas. The better developed your imagination is, the more creative you will be. Unfortunately you who don't love truth can and do use your imagination often to do what I call "imaginary living." You fantasize that you are not in control of yourself, suffering from some kind of illness, you have been abused, or you are a VICTIM of constant injustice. These imaginary circumstances justify your ill behavior in your estimation. You see how a person in denial will find a way to pretend everything is okay. In fact, pretending is an exact word to describe the lives of millions of people who suppress the truth in their own soul about life, truth, and their Creator.

This last one I will review is 'redefining.' It simply means that if you don't like what you hear, you give it a new definition. For example, "I don't fear, I'm just cautious or concerned," or, "I don't worry, I'm just watching out for my family." See, here you have re-defined fear and worry so that they are no longer the sin God says they are. In fact, you've given them a good connotation. Another, "I don't love money; I just need plenty in case of an emergency, or a good deal comes along." Here you have redefined 'love' to mean need. A re-definer is not a clever person who has exceptional language skills. Usually he is only mimicking what he has heard others say or do. For example, you hear someone say they don't like something about you. You become angry, jealous, or bitter. But instead of admitting this and confessing it, as integrity would do, you declare yourself hurt or offended. So you might say, "That hurt me." You feel better about your anger because you call it hurt.

All these defense mechanisms are all about self, self-preservation, self-esteem, self-promotion, self-justification, and many self words that put you at the center of your love and attention. Obsession with self is definitely at the root of all denial and defense. Obsession with your self-integrity is the solution to reverse your course and free yourself to enjoy life. You see, there is good and bad obsession.

Obsession with yourself is also called self-absorption. This state of mind puts blinders on you. Have you ever seen blinders on a horse to keep it from being distracted or spooked by external activity? These blinders give the horse tunnel vision, and so it is with self-absorption. You are focusing only on your own agenda. You are UNAWARE of your effect on others and you are unaware of your own error. You have blocked it all out through selective thinking. Ps. 36:2 says it this way, "For in his own eyes he flatters himself too much to DETECT or hate his own sin." Now this verse is loaded. When you deny truth about yourself, then you elevate ("flatter") yourself above the truth. This is self-absorption with blinders in place. As such you can not "detect" the real state of your life-you love yourself too much to "hate your own sin." The principle could go like this:

P. Deception resulting from denial and defense deadens your discernment.

You become unaware of your own fault.

Deception

Propaganda, brain-washing, and using a goal to justify a means are all ways of persuading people to believe something that they ordinarily would not. That is, to believe something that is not logical, rational, just, moral, or possibly even something

Denial, Defense, and Deception

that is not TRUE. This kind of persuasion can come from many sources: family, friends, government, school, churches, preachers, teachers, or even from the TV! When you do believe something that is not true, we call this deception. You are deceived. You think something is true or valuable when in fact it is not. You are blind in part to reality, you are convinced of your position, you have a blind spot.

This kind of deception happens on a small and large scale. Large scale, for example, is when many people believe a lie. There is plenty of religious and political history to demonstrate this. You might think of this as 'mass' deception. Then there is an individual personal deception when you are personally persuaded about something that is untrue. Someone may deceive you from a TV, a book, a classroom, or a pulpit, but a person often deceives himself. Now why would you believe something that is a lie? OR, why would you not believe something that is true? Well, you have just recently read why. It is called denial. When you deny a truth, then you will accept a lie. This is a natural law. Like gravity and death, you can not escape it. It means that if you will not believe the truth about yourself, then you will believe a lie about yourself (as well as about everything else important).

It is also a natural law that when you deny truth then you will take action to defend your action. As we have seen already, this defense includes justifying yourself, BUT the process does not stop there. This is very important to remember, that is, this process of self-justifying, over the course of time, leads to self-deception. You actually begin to believe you ARE right. You have convinced yourself. Others can convince you if you let them, or you can convince yourself. This is a human phenomena that reveals a weakness of the mind, a weakness that is not inevitable or natural, but is developed to the degree to which you have rejected truth, devalued truth, chosen to remain ignorant of truth, or simply insist on a numb apathy. Why? Because once truth is in you and you love it then it prevents the weakness that allows deception to develop.

Earlier in this paper I listed for you several ways people often say "not guilty." Regardless of how you might verbalize your innocence, when you do, when you are lying, you are putting yourself in a position to become deceived. Certainly you have known situations in which you would think, "How could he possibly believe that or live that way?" "How could people be so cruel to others?" "How can some people be so racial, greedy, excessive, obsessive, unjust, and extreme?" "How could anyone live on this creation and not know there is a Creator" Well, now you know, if you follow. Deception results in some very strange and anti-social behavior. Strange, that is, to those who are NOT deceived. A person of integrity who confesses his error and loves the truth is automatically protected from deception. He can NOT be deceived. His mind, soul, and LIFV (see glossary) are strong.

God the Holy Spirit puts it this way, "If we say that we have no sin, we are deceiving ourselves and the truth is not in us" (1 Jn. 1:8). Look carefully at this verse. To say you have "no sin" is denial. To say it and keep saying it is self-justification, which leads to, we are deceiving ourselves," that is, self-deception. You are convinced you are right. Now, how about this phrase, "the truth is not in us,"? Two points to note here are these. One, the love for the truth (integrity) being weak or absent is the REASON you denied your error. Then, low integrity is also the end result of your denying and defending, meaning the more truth you deny the more truth there is missing from your integrity pool. Let me put it this way, a lack of love for the truth leads to a lack of truth in you. As truth is denied residence in your soul, room is provided for a fake substitute. When a lie takes residence in your soul then you are deceived by it.

Denial, Defense, and Deception

Deception is a trap. It will hold you captive as a slave. Your freedom to think, imagine, create, explore, and advance is limited. Before you were deceived you were free to consider all things, think thoroughly about the good and bad of everything, or the value of any thing-what you see, hear, read, believe, or dream and to filter all this through your FOR. But now you can not do this without some impairment. This is the power of deception. It destroys a perfect awareness of reality. When you refuse to confess, forgive, or love the truth you give up your freedom, you abuse your LIFV, you reduce your integrity, and to illustrate, you step into a mold and pour concrete around yourself so you are frozen into position. Now only a jackhammer, a wrecking ball, or dynamite could budge you!

Bear with me as I remind you again that when you are confronted with something about yourself, your position, your belief, your family, or anything else you are attached to and what you hear is not what you like, or contradicts what you think, then this challenge is a TEST of your integrity. If what you hear is true, or is even possibly true but you reject or react to it then you enter denial and you fail the test and hurt your integrity. Reject truth about anything and you enter a rigid position of deception. You darken your life. You might think you are the defender of your faith and family or that you are being loyal in your zeal to reject any and every thing that might reveal fault with the things you love but actually you are probably starting a pattern in your life. This pattern of behavior suits you because it makes you feel good about yourself, so you do it again, and again until a pattern you develop. A pattern you are proud of! Deception is powerful. It's like getting an infection. The weak area of your integrity opens the door to this infiltration. You allow it, you give over your volition-you surrender it to error. This is abuse of your volition. Then you rationalize your bad choice in self-justification-this is abuse of your intelligence. This all happened because you abused your love—you love yourself (or others) more then you love truth. Is there abuse of faith here also? You bet there is. A person of faith does not live by sight, he or she lives by the unseen-integrity, God, and the life of faith. Therefore, deception is a result of the abuse of your basic soul functions (LIFV) and it is a powerful cause of soul dysfunction. Your life, even your mental capacity, become restricted, near-sighted, unaware, oversensitive, dependent, fearful, and short on purpose. You lose interest, motivation, and progress in things important. You busy yourself with everything else.

The Old Vicious Cycle

Take denial, defense, and deception and write them in a circle-or a cycle. This cycle spirals downward as it goes round and round. It is all a pattern as noted earlier that is revolving and rotating to build momentum and to build strength in its effect on your LIFV. Deception neutralizes your conscience because you think you are right. Therefore your conscience does not step in to interfere and stop the cycle. Now you are "free" to become an expert at defense of yourself. This position of pseudo-strength takes time to develop. It develops in a person or a culture. Just think of the things which are readily socially acceptable today, things of music, clothing, sexual behavior, marriage, divorce, language, or child behavior that would have one or two generations ago been embarrassing, insulting, or shameful. These changes in culture and personal behavior are NOT the result of evolution but are the result of that downward spiral. You see, this negative behavior pattern can be passed on to your children!

Because denial, defense, and deception are so connected in a process, all three will be mentioned throughout this text. Let me give you a historical example and further analysis. Jesus said to Pilate, "Whoever is on the side of truth (loves truth) comes to ME" (Jn. 18:37). Pilate took this as an invitation and challenge to his integrity-a test. He used a DM to defend his position-to

Denial, Defense, and Deception

stay mentally and spiritually exactly where he wanted to be; no where! Pilate said, "What is truth?" People who don't want to come to the truth say this same thing in many ways. For example, "There is no absolute truth." "There are many truths." "That's your opinion." "I have a right to my own opinion." "How can anyone know for sure?" Pilate is an example of many who refuse absolute truth. He denies it and rejects it. How does he excuse himself? He or you excuse yourself from responsibility by simply claiming that there is NO standard of behavior by which you can be judged. This is very common, if not the most common, form of denial in our world today. You see, most of the world lives in denial of absolute truth (see *Orientation to Life*). This means they reject (deny) God's standard. Why? Because when there is no standard there can be no expectation then there can be no violation. For example, all the ball team decides to play by everyone's own rules, and then there will be no errors!

Let me say this another way. Some defense mechanisms, in effect, say I did not break the rules, standards, or the truth (synonyms). Other DM's say I am not subject to those rules-yours, God's, or others. Then this last category says there are no rules, at least, none that I accept or agree with. These three categories of response to truth pretty much cover all the ways people in denial defend themselves. Let us review to be explicit.

1. I did not violate the rules or truth.

2. I am not subject to any such rule or truth.

3. I do not believe in any such rule or truth.

All three of these are denial and all three involve the use of defense mechanisms-to defend your innocence-to self justify.

Here are some Biblical examples of denial and defense (DM's). Study these and see which DM is used. Remember, a DM is a type of human solution.

Gen. 3:11-12	Adam Blames Eve
Gen. 3:13	Eve blames the serpent
Gen. 4:5-8	Cain rejects God's appeal to him
Gen. 4:9-10	Cain lies about his sin
Gen. 16:5	In denial, Sarai becomes jealous and vindictive
Lk. 18:9-14	Self-righteous deception is a trap
Jn. 8:31-38	Denial leads to false security and deception
Jn. 8:42-44	The Father of denial
Jude 8	Denial rejects authority
Lk. 10:25-29	Bad love leads to self-justification

This passage in Lk. 10:25-29 is the historical narrative of what may be the most outstanding personal experience Jesus had with an individual who proactively tried to justify self. He was a knowledgeable and religious person, he could quote Scripture, and even answered correctly Jesus' question about life. But see in verse 29 there is a revelation about what was in his heart. God looks at the heart (1 Sam. 16:7). He wanted to "justify himself." Please read this passage in Luke. He knew there were people he did NOT love. Rather than confess this heart condition, repent, change, obey, and become like God-to improve his integrity, he chose to deny then defend himself. How did he do this? He used a DM which could be called "Ignorance." "I don't understand the truth." "It's not clear to me." "It needs interpretation." "Who is my neighbor?" "Define neighbor."

Do you get my point here? He hides behind any of these human excuses to self justify no compliance and disobedience.

Denial, Defense, and Deception

So Jesus gave him an illustration of neighbor to make it clear as crystal, that is to make it UNDENIABLE! This is the power of God's word (Heb. 4:12). It will expose and destroy all fake concepts and human denials. The historical record of deception here on earth begins in the Garden of Eden. Eve was deceived by Satan. She turned away from what God had told her. She rejected and denied it, freeing herself to possibly satisfying her own desires. Had she been committed to truth she would not have been deceived. To feel free to get something she wanted she needed to believe a lie, so she did.

Today, man's nature perpetuates deception. He naturally seeks that which is outside of God's will, opening himself up to deception. Satan promotes this process because he chose to rebel against God's will and is His enemy. Jesus called him "the father of lies" in Jn. 8:44. When he contorts a lie for you and you believe it, you are deceived by him. When you create a lie about yourself (such as your innocence) then you deceive yourself. To be brief, if you study the historical course of mankind and were to report it on the front page of a universal newspaper, the headline might go something like this:

Deception Sharply Increases Despite Maximum Revelation

Paul predicted deception would become much worse in spite of the fact that God has revealed more to us, a lot more. The word of God is available in print, on CD's, DVD's, in many languages, on-line, radio, TV, and has been spread verbally by many people in many ways to many places for many centuries. But, in spite of this Paul said,

"But evil men and imposters will proceed from bad to worse, deceiving, and being deceived" (II Tim. 3:13). Evil men and imposters are those who are deceived. They are deceived because they denied the truth, lived in denial, justified it, and now are self deceived. Deceived people become pawns and promoters. In deception, they seek company to support their position and feel comfort. This company today is very large and it has a lot of momentum. The world is darker now because as Jesus said in Jn. 3:18, "men love darkness." It will become so dark that He also said that when He returns He would not find "faith" in this world (Lk. 18:8). Faith and love for the truth (integrity) will become more scarce, but His return is even more certain.

This is the future of deception, that is, destruction. Jesus Christ, who is the truth, will return to end all deception. It is written:

"And I saw heaven opened, and behold, a white horse, and he who sat on it is called Faithful and True, and in righteousness He judges and wages war" (Revelations 19:11). At this point His will will be done on Earth as it is in heaven (sound familiar?). "And then the devil who deceived them (from Eve till the end) was thrown into the lake of fire . . ." (Rev. 20:10).

More Synonyms

I could not finish this subject without saying something about hypocrisy. Why? Because this was the definitive label Jesus himself most often gave those who rejected and denied Him. They defended themselves skillfully and they were deceived. He said they could neither "see" nor "hear" the truth. This is a product of deception. Hypocrisy resulted. Why? Because some parts of the truth they needed to profess for their own benefit-to appear loyal and religious to others. In fact, the use of religion to "white wash" one's image is one of the most worn out defense mechanisms in the world. Yet in their hearts-where God looks-they did not love the truth. They were pretenders (another synonym). This lifestyle is also called duplicity (yet another synonym). Duplicity is simply a double life, double standard, or double-minded (Js. 1:7-8).

An example of unbelievers who were living this way is found in Titus 1:10-16. Note in verse 14, some had "turned away from the truth." This is denial. They were unbelieving (v. 15) and they "professed to know God but by their deeds they DENY Him"

Denial, Defense, and Deception

(v. 16). Does it surprise you that there are unbelievers who profess to know God? Well, it might also surprise them to know that they do NOT know God. Why? Because they are deceived.

There are several warnings from God-your Creator-to not be deceived, meaning it is possible to maintain integrity. This warning is to "watch out," "be on the alert," "be sober (aware)" of the fact that you are the target of enemies that would like to neutralize you.

For example, the book of Revelation, using several Greek word forms for deception, primarily the word "planos," does so 91 times! Revelation (meaning that it was written to REVEAL to you information which would prevent deception) 3:14-19 addresses people who were NOT "sober". Note especially v. 17 which states their real condition. They "say" they are in good condition. They "do not know they are in bad condition. Now, when you believe you are living well, when in fact you are living poorly, this is called being dec _ _ _ ed. I must repeat myself. Now hear this-these are believers (v. 14, 19) who thought that because of their blessings and comfortable life, God was pleased with them. They were deceived by their own material success . . . worldly success. Jesus said to them that they needed to "be zealous and repent" (v. 19).

This word "repent" leads to a passage which will give you insight to a basic principle, that is, the method that produces deception AND the procedure to prevent deception. This is found in I Jn. 1:6-10. You must read it and have it with you to go further. Now, notice right off that duplicity factor again. You say one thing but do another. This means that what is in your heart does not agree with what comes from your mouth. You say you have "fellowship with him" but you "walk in darkness." God is not in darkness. You are in darkness, so there can be no fellowship, that is, cooperation and confidence. And why is the word "darkness" used? Because as light represents God and truth, darkness represents the opposite. Evidence of "walking in darkness" is that you will say whatever you please to satisfy yourself. When you do this you "lie and do not practice the truth" (v.6). Lying and not practicing the truth is a definition of de_ _al. Good . . . I mean bad!

Please notice in these verses there are four sentences. Each one starts with the phrase, "If we." If you do something positive or negative then there IS a consequence. That is, each time you use your volition (V), you choose good or bad, better or worse then you benefit or lose depending on your choice. Denial, defense, and deception ALL depend on volition. The second statement of John is, "if you say that you have NO sin you are deceiving yourself and the truth is not in you" (v 8). Truth-lovers are people of integrity. This protects them from deception. But if you deny your sin or your error, you reject this protection and you will eventually believe a lie-about yourself, someone, some belief, some church, or anything you overvalue. Note also from the last sentence in v. 10 that, "if you say you have not sinned, you make Him a liar and His word is not in you. "

This is serious. To deny your sin not only weakens you and reduces you to self deception, it also has an effect on God Himself. You are in effect saying that you are right and God (truth, light, word) is wrong! He is a liar because you are not. You cannot both be right about your behavior. Guess who first in history called God a liar? He put it this way, "Has God said . . . you surely will not die"(Gen. 3:1-4). When you call God a liar like he did then you support his position (see *Angelic Conflict*). You become a witness for your defense and for his-the enemy of God!

Let me stop and give you a couple of examples to clarify what I am saying. If you say to someone, "You hurt my feelings," when in fact you know they only told you the truth, then you are not "practicing the truth, you are saying you have "no sin". If you live a life professing to love God and yet you resent some people for

Denial, Defense, and Deception 95

any reason, you are deceived. If you hold anyone in contempt because they do not agree or cooperate with you, you are making God a liar! The good news from this passage is that God has not left you without prevention of deception nor without a cure for it. Verse seven states clearly that if you will "walk in the light" you will maintain all relationship (R) and the blood of Jesus will provide the cleaning of your life from sin. "Walk in the Light" is a metaphor for a lifestyle of Integrity. Furthermore verse nine PROMISES that if you will confess your sins, He is faithful and righteous to forgive you your sins and to cleanse you from all unrighteousness. Key word—confess, confess, confess.

Types of Deception

As Eve was deceived by Satan even so many people are today. This is 'external' deception. You who deny your own personal bad behavior deceive yourself, this is self deception. This is 'internal' deception. You accept the external and it becomes internal. Some external sources of deception are culture, politics, tradition, religion, angels, and people. These are sources and types of deception. In addition, these have many methods to deceive. Disguise, decoy, distraction, and deterrent are used to mislead you. Jesus said there are "wolves in sheep's clothing" (Matthew 7:15). Paul wrote this warning in II Cor. 11:13-15. Satan and his helpers are disguised as messengers of light. This means you may not know who is who and what is what. Especially since "there is a way (belief) which SEEMS RIGHT to a man but the end is death" (Prov. 14:12). This is another warning from God that you are prone to deception. Your disadvantage does have a solution. But you must PURSUE it. "Walk in the Light" means love the truth, think and learn the truth, believe the truth, and always choose truth over anything in this world. Did you see I just listed your LIFV?

I have stated earlier that deception can take place by 1. Telling and teaching lies, 2. Withholding truth, or 3. Both. Now, recall the history of truth as it has been revealed to you by your Creator.

The greatest revelation of truth came through Jesus Christ when He revealed to you the "words" and person of God Himself. All this was recorded and is now contained in the Bible. The Bible's arch enemy began an immediate deception strategy based on the three methods listed above. He inspired many to develop their own personal doctrine about the written Word. He inspired the government to adopt the Bible as its religion, but mix it with pagan religion. Then he inspired this powerful religious organization to withhold the written word of God from the population while it substituted a lot of its own ritual and religion. For over 1,000 years this "church" successfully withheld scripture and its translation and distribution. Over time and at the cost of their own lives some men of integrity translated, printed, promoted, and taught the contents of Scripture to the world. A victory over deception and ignorance was won. So Satan responded by promoting not one religion but 'one thousand', so to speak. His desire and ploy is for there to be a church on every corner and a personal religion for every person. This strategy promotes diversity, chaos, confusion, disagreement, division, strife, and disunity which is a negative. His goal through this means is to show that there is NO unified absolute truth.

However, do not be deceived by this. This diversity is only the APPEARANCE of things. The fact is that God's Word itself declares that there is only ONE truth. Ephesians 4:5 says there is only, "one Lord, one faith, and one baptism . . ." One God has one truth in one book and it has been that way without change, error, or re-write, or redefinition since nearly 2,000 years! The principle of One, All, and None is throughout Scripture, what does this mean? It is like a natural law, for example, gravity-one force has its effect on all matter with no exceptions. Fire is always light and never dark. There are laws created by God in the natural world He created. There are also laws created by God in the spiritual world that preceded this visible world. One of the laws is the law of 'OAN' (One, All, and None). God is ONE, He created

Denial, Defense, and Deception 97

ALL, and there are NONE besides Him. This is absolute. All truth is one truth, created by one God; there is NO truth outside of this. Man cannot create truth or create God because man is created. All creatures must discover all truth from one God. There are spiritual laws. Human diversity and religions, inspired and promoted by Satan to divide believers, weaken them, and deceive them are violations of God's laws. DO NOT participate!

Seeing, But NOT Believing

Trying to break some natural laws, like gravity, can be quite painful! And so nature is meant through its many illustrations to teach us about the eternal, the spiritual. Try breaking God's spiritual laws and this too has a destructive effect on your soul. We even have idioms for the condition of your serial violations. For example, you may hear, "he can't see past the nose on his face," or "he can't see the forest for the trees," or, "he has tunnel vision." You often mean by those that someone is unable to see (hear or believe) the OBVIOUS (Matt. 11:16-17, Lk. 12:54-56).

Here is a brief conversation to illustrate what I mean. 'B' says, "You mean you really believe the Bible?" 'A' says, "Why yes," 'B' says, "But why?" 'A' says, "Well, the Bible says God created the heavens and the earth and guess what? Every day I get up and go out and there they are! The Bible says that everyone is a sinner, and the penalty for sin is death. Lo and behold, I look around and every person is dying, without exception. God said in the Bible that the Messiah would come, and He did. He said people would reap what they sow and they do. He said faith in Christ would result in a new birth, and it does. Shall I go on?

Jesus spoke of this condition of mental dullness. He said these have eyes to see but cannot see, and ears to hear but cannot hear. This is a blindness and deafness to truth that DEVELOPS when you insist on your own will and way in life. In your determination (denial) to have your own life, you ASSIGN VALUE to things as you wish. You may even assign high value to religion, tradition, ritual, or a denominational sect. Perhaps you did this because others; family, friends, or peers did it, so you are simply conforming.

Having assigned value to whatever it is that attracts you, you give yourself to it. You love it. You are self-satisfied and further motivated to PERSIST in it and INSIST on it. Now, if you believe in GOD, you may even think He is quite satisfied with your tenacity. Alas, this is the condition of many mis-guided souls. Go back to the beginning. Re-evaluate the value of all things with reference to what God values-revealed in His Word. Remember that even though you can be deceived about what is obvious, if you are pursuing integrity then you are NOT likely to be deceived by what APPEARS to be right, or imitation, or a counterfeit.

Too Complex

You might get a headache reading this. Deception can be very complex. It is tricky because this is its goal-to trick you. Now if you will read this carefully you will see the sense of it but it is revealing of how you can be tricked by focusing on one aspect of what you do or think you believe while being blind to any other aspect of it. What are the aspects? First is the aspect of 'method'. The word "way" means method.

1. A wrong thing done in a wrong way is wrong.

2. A wrong thing done in a right way is wrong.

3. A right thing done in a wrong way is wrong.

ONLY

4. A right thing done in a right way is right.

Next, is the aspect of motive:

1. A wrong thing done with a wrong motive is wrong.

Denial, Defense, and Deception

2. A wrong thing done with a right motive is wrong.

3. A right thing done with a wrong motive is wrong.

ONLY

4. A right thing done with a right motive is right.

Then the third aspect is the thing itself. All this means is simply this. The thing you do or believe has to be right and true. This is the 'what'. The thing has to be done with the right method-done properly. This is the 'how'. And the thing has to be done with the right 'motive'. This is the 'why' you do it or believe it. Because anyone or two, or three of these aspects could be wrong you could be deceived-unaware that you are out of line as to the truth, and as to what God values. Absolutely everything that you can think, believe, speak, or do can possibly be wrong. This is the human condition. In spite of how well established, traditional, historical, or pleasant it is, it can possibly be wrong, done wrong, or done with wrong motive. And you, as well as anyone else, could possibly be deceived about it. That is, you MIGHT be wrong about what you are really comfortable with. It is a weakness of human nature. This is precisely why God has to tell us in Scripture, "Do not be deceived . . ." (1 Cor. 6:9, 15:33, Gal. 6:7, Js. 1:16, 2 Thess. 2:3, Eph.5:6, 1 Cor. 3:18).

Jesus Christ said that deceivers and deception will evolve. It will become more powerful. "For false Christs and false prophets will arise and will show great signs and wonders, so as to mislead (deceive), if possible, even the elect" (Matthew 24:24). This is your future environment if not your present. It means that some very convincing people who can perform some very persuasive activities are likely to deceive you if you are not careful. What does this prophecy and deception about eternal truth have to do with your personal life of being honest with yourself and others? I am glad you asked. The answer is everything. When you deceive yourself through poor personal integrity then you become the fool who will fall for anything. You are easily fooled, misled, and deceived by all that is persuasive, pleasant, and popular.

Let me tell you that rooting out deception takes some mental work. How can you be sure you are not deceived about something, anything? Examine yourself. Examine the three aspects listed above. What you do, think, and value has to be authorized or allowed by God. Do they adjust to His will and Word? Have you looked to see? Does what you are practicing improve your integrity? All that is important is authorized or unauthorized by God's Word-the Truth.

The second factor is about method. Are you using a method, procedure, or plan that is fair and honest. It uses no one and is considerate of everyone. It adjusts it self to God's will, character, and therefore is impartial and not forceful. You know that the end does NOT justify the means. The means must always be a right method. So the third factor is your motive. Only you and God know your heart. Why do you do or believe what you do? Hopefully not for attention, not for pleasing others, and not for personal ambition. All that you do must have a motive of God's character. Love is the ultimate motive, love for God and your neighbor. Gain is not a right motive because it focuses on self. It is very easy to slip into self-serving motives. That is because it is human and it is promoted by humans. Beware in this area. Many people think that they are doing great work, but actually have wrong motives.

The passage of Scripture that explains these principles to you, leaving no doubt as to the value of right motives is 1 Cor. 13:1-3. Paul says in short, ". . . if I give all my possessions, even my own body, and do not have the right motive of love, I am nothing" (paraphrase). In other words, love is the right motive, not romantic love, not loyalty, not bad love, but love that is godly, selfless, and fully defined by verses 4-7. In summary, Paul says in 1 Cor. 16:14, "Let ALL that you do be done in love." This will protect you from deception. But remember, good love is love that has the right object (read *Good and Bad Principle*).

Thing, method, and motive correspond to what, how, and why. Go back to the analysis I gave you. Draw one circle around the words "thing" in each of the four lines. Do the same with the words "method" and "motive". Remember these, so that, when you hear about a government policy, a church endeavor, or a personal project, the real and lasting true value of what you hear about will depend on these three points: what it is, how it is done, and why it is done-the thing, the method, and the motive. Here is a notable related warning from your Creator. "Let no man deceive himself. If any man among you THINKS that he is wise in this age, he must become foolish, so that he may become wise. For the wisdom of this world is foolishness before God. For it is written 'He is the one who catches the wise in their craftiness,' and again, 'The Lord knows the reasoning's of the wise, that they are useless.' So then let no one boast in men." (1 Cor. 3: 18-21).

Before I leave this trilogy, or trinity, I would like to give you my personal opinion of the primary subject of each of these three factors:

1. Thing or what - the essence of God.

2. Method, or how - the plan of salvation.

3. Motive, or why - the love for God and your neighbor.

Divine Solution

Prevention of and solution to deception is to focus on and pursue the truth. This is the important principle-the more you focus on what IS in the Word of God, the less you will value what is NOT in His Word. This is primarily true for the things that God's Word disapproves but it is also true for things that are purely human, worldly, and temporal. You see, to overvalue something is to love it and to be captured by something traps you in deception. You really believe in the value of it when, in fact, it is minimal.

Don't be shocked or offended by this list of examples I am giving here. It is a fact that they are NOT in Scripture. Remember that the will of God is in the Word of God. Examples of the human, worldly, and temporal: health, family unity, church membership, popularity, possessions, professional progress, personal skills and talents. These things are highly valued among people. This is exactly why they carry the risk of self-deception. All of this list has some dependence on human behavior, and everything that depends on human behavior is NOT dependable. Jesus Himself said that He did not come to bring peace but a sword to divide-a son from his father, mother from daughter, and etc. (Lk. 12:51-53). This is because people AND the things they create (traditions, doctrines, rituals) are not always in line with God's will, plan, or truth. So, if you chose people over truth when they oppose the truth you will become deceived. If you chose truth over people who prefer their own way then you become divided. This is good division.

Sources of Deception

If you were going to a dangerous location to stay for awhile and I could tell you six ways that you could most likely get hurt or harmed there, you would probably listen up. In fact, you might even jot them down so as not to forget, so you could stay on your guard. Well guess what? You are living in that dangerous place and there are at least six sources of deception awaiting you at all times. These sources are also the six sources of evil. Deception is a type of evil, and all evil originates ultimately from the Deceiver. These six sources are:

1. Self. Self-deception is internal. You do this to yourself, primarily by apathy or denying truth.

Denial, Defense, and Deception

2. Cosmic. The world's deception is external. It attracts you and you expose yourself to it more or less, often because you think it is harmless.

3. Cultural. Another external type of deception that influences you through peer pressure, tradition, language, definitions, and majority power. The more you value your culture, the more opportunity it has to deceive you.

4. Religion. This internal and external source is difficult to expose, escape, or even explain. It is often like a stew. Many ingredients are added and some are very good. Then there are those add-ins that are poison to you. Because it is mixed with the good, it deceives you, sort of like "yeast" in bread, or like "tares" mixed in the "wheat" (Matt. 13:24-43).

5. Demonic or Angelic. This external source is an actual invisible person who can control you or possess you so that you are motivated by his or her values to do his or her goals. The deceived person is vulnerable to what he is unaware of.

6. People. This external source is the visible persons who attempt to do the same as the last category, that is, to manipulate and use you. You submit and follow because you become convinced they are right, or at least they are important to you.

Deception TARGETS all four functions of the soul (LIFV). Abuse of these functions will result ultimately in deception about what has true value and what are the true solutions to life problems and needs. For example, you might love (L) the wrong objects or people while you think these are the right ones. You begin to think (I) things that are not logical, but you are unable to be aware of this illogical thinking. You follow the crowd and put your trust (F) in some human system, or people themselves, convinced that this is security. You reach a satisfaction with all your own choices (V) because you believe you are FREE to make them yourself.

Deception is an arrogance role in which you are self-satisfied, content, and determined with YOUR choices, values, and beliefs. You may not be content in the absolute sense. In fact, you are even "reaping" from poor choices, but you insist on contentment in those choices and beliefs, that is, you will NOT change, submit, or learn better. This IS the opposite of integrity. This is arrogance!

Salient Summary Points

1. Denial, Defense, and Deception will result in various symptoms: stress, anxiety, and depression (SAD). Frustration, loneliness, discouragement, disillusionment, disappointment, conflict, and contest.

2. Biblical synonyms for deny or denial: harden, hardens, hardened, reject, turn, lie, darkness. Biblical antonyms: confess and confession, turn, truth, light.

3. There is good and bad denial. Good denial is denial of self and excess for the benefit of others or your own integrity. Good denial is right denial of any untruth about you or about life and God. Bad denial is denial of truth about anything or any person.

4. There is good and bad defense. Good defense is the honest and truthful defense against attack on you which is untrue and undeserved. Bad defense is the behavior you use to justify a position of innocence when in fact you are not innocent. It is also bad when you defend a decision to reject what you know to be true.

5. There is no good and bad deception. All deception is bad. You may observe from the Divine life, all there is is

Denial, Defense, and Deception

good. From the human life, all there is has good and bad, then from the Satan's life all there is is bad. The origin of deception is Satan. Therefore it is all bad. (Remember the *One, All, and None principle?* This is an example of it.)

6. Biblical synonyms for deception: falsehood, false lie, mirror, sheep's clothing, white-washed, hypocrite, double-minded, deceit, guile, counterfeit, blind, darkness, dead.

7. Most commonly used defense mechanism: projection. It is similar to blaming. Adam blamed Eve. Pilate said, "His blood be on YOUR hands." And he said, "I AM INNOCENT . . ." (Matt. 21: 24).

8. There are three ways you are misled and deceive others. One is to tell and persuade them of a lie. One is to tell only part of the truth resulting in wrong conclusions on their part. One is to with-hold information they need. This is why we demand in court that one tell the truth, the whole truth, and nothing but the truth. A defendant can do this in court, a teacher can do this in class, and a spouse can do this to a partner.

9. To pursue the Integrity of God means to:

    a. Hear, believe, and obey (HBO) the ONE truth He has provided you.

    b. To accept ALL truth about ALL things and people, and to love ALL truth.

    c. This results in having NO deception, denial, defense, duplicity, or double standards in you.

This is commanded clearly in Eph. 4:20-25.

10. God knows who is in denial and deception. He knows how deep and strong it is in you. He knows what it would take to break you out of it (Matt. 11:16-24, Jn. 4:7-10).

11. Beware of music, talent, skill, intellect, personality, and all things attractive and impressive. Why? Because those are good when associated with truth and integrity, right methods and motives, but they are bad if used to promote self, error, poor values, or simply to profit.

12. Beware of deception through terminology. Example:

    a. God. This name was respected as the one true Biblical God. Now it is used for everything that surprises you, or it is used for any god your imagination creates.

    b. Religion. This word was used to describe Biblical belief and faith. Now it is used for anyone's personal creation of anything of faith.

    c. Christian. Originally meant a person who loves and follows Jesus Christ and His words in the Bible. Now used by many as a label for any minor or moral association with His name.

13. You ask what does personal denial of truth about self have to do with deception about God's truth? Good question. Answer-everything. They both have a common denominator-love for the truth. You may know some truth, but do you love it? Do you pursue it?

14. Jesus said, "If you continue (pursuit) in My Word, then you are truly disciples of Mine; and you will know the truth, and the truth will make you FREE" (Free from slavery, deception, and ignorance.) Jn. 8:31-32.

"A Name Gone Vain"
A test of your integrity

Jesus prayed, "Father, glorify your name." This prayer of Jesus Christ is one of a kind. The entire prayer is recorded in Jn. 12:27-28. It is very short and contains only one request. Most unique about this prayer is that it is the only one recorded for us that has an audible answer from our Father in heaven to Jesus Christ. This is not the only time He spoke from heaven for all to hear but it is the only time He spoke in response to a prayer request from earth.

Therefore, we ought to pay particular attention to the request of the prayer. What is important to Christ should be important to you, His disciple. To value and love what He values and loves is, in fact, a definition of integrity. Jesus Christ is requesting that God the Father glorify His NAME. Therefore, you should want God's NAME to be glorified. It is your responsibility to adjust your life so that you desire and pursue what is important to God. It is important to God that His NAME be glorified.

How is God's name glorified? He does this by revealing His divine and superior character to the world. The key word here is, "revealing", that is, making known more about Himself. On the other hand, you glorify God's name by "reflecting" in your behavior and speech what you think about God. If you love God and think He is a PERSON worthy of all your worship and adoration, then you will reflect this in the way you obey Him and the way you talk about Him, even the way you use HIS NAME. That is, you will glorify His NAME. To glorify means to hold in great esteem, respect, awe, and even obligation. To honor and celebrate His NAME. To elevate it to a high position of priority. Why? Because this NAME represents the One who you love with all your mind, heart, and soul. No NAME therefore deserves the careful use that this One does.

Think of who you love on this earth. Do you use their name at the drop of a hat? To express surprise or shock, or to "call" on their name as a way of expressing your emotion? I ask you to evaluate how you use the NAME of God because it is the name above all names that demands your respect. God is a Person, not an expression. When you show to the world that you respect God's name through judicious use of it, then you testify to them your faith that God is real, and that He has your attention.

The Death of a Name

Apparently, the name of God is quite important. God even talks about His own NAME in many passages of the Old Testament. One of those names, the first, in fact, that He recorded is Elohim (Gen. 1). This name, as special as it was, unfortunately began to be used by people randomly and injudiciously for any god they pleased. Gods that were created by people, gods that were fake, and especially gods that were entirely different in character from the God of the Bible were being given the name Elohim.

Three Bible passages that record this historical fact are Genesis 35:1-4, Exodus 12:12, and Numbers 33:4. Where the word "gods" is in Hebrew the word Elohim. This is a quote from, *"The God of the Bible and other Gods"*, written by Robert P. Lightner, page 131. "These passages indicate three facts. First, the name Elohim was retained and used by people. Second, people began to forget the true meaning of the name. Third, Elohim thus became a meaningless term to them." This is a fitting illustration of the believer who retains the name Christian but whose life contradicts the real meaning of that name!

"A Name Gone Vain"

You must understand that a name, a term, or a word will lose its TRUE meaning and its intended importance or effect when over a period of time it is used improperly, when it is used without discrimination and when it is in fact finally redefined. This is a weakness of language.

As a matter of fact, this process of destruction of the usefulness of the name of God has taken place, and continues to take place today. This has happened to the word Christian, as suggested by Dr. Lightner. It has also happened to the word religion (see *Religion of Life*). The word truth has also been re-defined and diluted (see *Full Coverage and Full Disclosure*). Now, the name of God is our concern. His NAME began to be so abused, misused, and misrepresented by everyone and anyone that it no longer existed as a NAME which did "glorify" Him. That is it did not represent, define, and distinguish the God of the Bible in the minds of the speakers and hearers.

So guess what God did about this? He did three things that I can discover. One, He gave to mankind another name for Himself. Yahweh is the primary one He gave (Ex. 6:3). Then He passed a law. This law is first recorded in Exodus 20:7, and is referred to as the third commandment. It says, "You shall not take the name of the Lord your God in vain, for the Lord will not leave him unpunished who takes His name in vain". Now the word "vain" means useless, worthless, and self-serving. The name Elohim had been used "in vain". It had been used for creatures and false gods. When a name is used "in vain" it is being used improperly to the point that it loses its true meaning and its intended effect. God did not and does not want this to happen to His name, so He passed a law. Furthermore, He is so serious about this that He also gives a warning of punishment to those who use His name without respect.

Note that in all ten of the commandments in Exodus 20 and Deuteronomy 5 there are only two that promise punishment if they are not obeyed. This reflects a seriousness of the issue. The first three commandments are about your relationship with your Creator. First, you are not to have anyone (gods) more important to you than He is. Second, you are not to worship any of creation or anything created; only the Creator. This comes with a strong warning of punishment. Then the third commandment, our primary subject, which naturally follows the first two, that is, with a healthy respect for God—the number one love of your life—your Creator the ONE you worship, you will have a respect for His NAME that should prevent you from using it in a useless way. Furthermore, if you do take the name of the "Lord your God" in vain, this is evidence that your relationship is not right with Him.

Please read this short passage again. Jesus said, "Father, glorify your name." And His response was, "I have glorified it, and I will glorify it again" (Jn. 12:28). Note that this passage has the word glorify three times, the word name three times and uses all three tenses—past, present, and future. This is an observation which to me simply compounds the importance of what is said.

Adjustment is Necessary

Remember, at this point, what the problem is. The name of God is today being abused, misused, diluted, disrespected, degraded, dishonored, down-graded, redefined, demeaned, disgraced, and defamed. It is being made familiar, generic, impersonal, subjective, and unreal. This is a loss to God, to the church, and loss of witness to the world. This is all a result of using God's name "in vain".

For example, when you say, "O God, My God", "O Lord", or "Jesus" just because something surprises or impresses you, OR you use His NAME as an emotional reaction—good or bad—to make verbal expression of your emotion, this is "in vain". You have used God's name in vain. "In vain" does not mean profanity, it means "no value". Check your dictionary.

"A Name Gone Vain"

This behavior of yours creates loss to the value of the NAME of God. And if you have not noticed it, you should realize that you are talking just like the world is talking. This is worldliness—you have lost your witness to the world. You see, they hear you use the NAME of God the same way they do, therefore in their minds, their god is the same as yours! And what is that—He is not really a person, He is only an expression. Why, if someone or something impressed or depressed you, would you say "O mother", or "O George", or "O Lucy", or "Jack"? It makes no sense to use a real person's name known to you when they have nothing to do with the situation that provoked you to call out their name. Therefore, if you would not use a REAL person's name, then why use God's name. Is He not real?

Every time you speak God's name in a vain way, it is like giving the hearers a shot of Novocaine; they become more numb to His name. There is no reverent reaction as there should be. The principle is this: A name used "in vain" long enough will finally become vain (without effect). Please don't be a part of this process.

Listen, if God is real to you and you love Him AND you love what He loves then you will love His NAME and use it properly. Many of you are under "punishment" (discipline) now because you have joined the world in destroying the NAME of God. Then there are some of you who misuse His NAME, revealing that you don't really know Him as a real person anyway.

Hallow means What?

This third thing God did provides the final solution for all the problem. He came Himself to earth to demonstrate how you should treat His NAME. He said in Matthew 6:5, "When you pray . . . pray in this way, Our Father who is in heaven, Hallowed be Your NAME" (v9).

Notice that the Lord introduced this instruction by stating first in verses 5-8 a lot about how pagans and hypocrites were abusing the name of God. They were using the name of God for their own personal gain. The used it "in vain". Jesus said in verse 8, "So do not be like them . . ."

"Hallow" means just the opposite of vain. Hallow is an antonym of vain, and it is a synonym of glorify. Hallow means to hold in such high esteem as to exalt and even worship the NAME. It means to hold in great distinction as sacred and pure.

It means to put it above everything else so that all things are below it. This is the proper attitude toward the NAME of God. This right frame of mind about the name of God will prevent the wrong use of His name which robs Him of His right representation.

In this prayer of Matthew 6, Jesus Christ is telling you to pray that God's name be "hallowed". This assumes that you do it yourself. That is, you have to hallow the name of God before you can honestly pray that it will be hallowed.

Now notice that I am using another reference to prayer, and this is another unique prayer. It is one of a kind. It is the only prayer that Jesus taught people to pray—verses 9-13. The prayer starts with a concern about the Person of God the Father— His NAME. Where have we seen this already? Right. The Ten commandments start out with instructions about the Person of God. God is a Person, NOT a religion (see Religion or Life). A right attitude and relationship with God AND the name of God is the beginning of Life (see *Life*). Begin anything without respect for God and my friend, you are on your own. You were not created to be on your own and you are not free to use His NAME with impunity.

Example and Opportunity

First, the example. Job is a man that had the surprise and shock of such intensity most of us will never know anything like

"A Name Gone Vain"

it. Sudden loss, violent tragedy, and that beyond all natural odds that certainly many today would automatically say "O My God" or "O Lord". (Imagine how much of that was said at the tragedy of 911!) Yet, this man because of his INTEGRITY (Job 2:3) did not use God's name in vain. Instead, he used it to say something true about God AND to BLESS His name. (Now you have three synonyms: glorify, hallow, and bless). Listen to what Job said when he heard the news of all his loss.

"The LORD gave and the LORD has taken away. Blessed be the NAME of the Lord" (Job 1 :21). Verse 22 says that Job did not sin. One way in which he did not sin is that he did not use God's name in vain. His personal integrity and his love for God prevented any misuse of God's name; in fact, just the opposite resulted he blessed the NAME of God!

Now for the opportunity part. I mentioned how the abuse of God's name has resulted in loss, loss of testimony and witness to the world, loss of the believer's identity as a person who loves God, and loss of fellowship with God because you are under "punishment" (Ex. 20:7). This loss is first regained by obeying command number 3 personally. Then you are ready to go further and minister to those who remain behind. That is, when someone—anyone—says to you God's name, ask them WHY did you mention His name? Is it because you believe God is a real person? Since you brought up the subject could I ask you what you think or believe about Him? May I tell you what I believe about Him?

I believe that He created us. He loved us. He died for our sins. He rose from the dead and is alive today. His name is Jesus Christ, and whoever believes in His NAME has eternal life (Jn. 3:16, 3:36, 5:24).

"But as many as received Him, to them He gave the right to become children of God, even to those who believe in His NAME . . ." Jn 1: 12).

Let me remind you that there is a coming reward for those who fear His NAME (see Rev. 11:18). Now you have 4 synonyms: glorify, hallow, bless, and fear; all toward the name of God!

"Who will not fear, O Lord, and glorify your name? For You alone are holy" (Rev. 15:4). Answer: Those who do not respect His name, but use it carelessly.

Principle: The respect with which you use God's name is a measure of your integrity.

Glossary

AROG: Arrogance

ATP: Anticipation

AWF: Anxiety, Worry, & Fear

C&C: Confidence & Courage

CPR: Contentment, Peace, & Rest

DG: Divine Good

DM: Divine Motivation

DV: Divine Viewpoint

FOL: Fear of Loss

G&B: Good and Bad Principle

H&H: Honesty & Humility

HG: Human Good

HM: Human Motivation

HV: Human Viewpoint

LIFV: Love, Intelligence, Faith, & Volition

LOF: Life of Faith

M&M: Motive & Method

PIP2: Primary Principles of Non-Possession & Contentment

PAWM: Priest, Ambassador, Witness, & Member of the Body of Christ

POD: Possession-Obsession Disorder

PPP: Push-Pull Principle

PSD: Personal Sense of Destiny

RIR2: Right Thing Done in Right Way

RPD: Relationship, Purpose, & Destiny

SAD: Stress, Anxiety, & Depression

SS: Serial Sinning

TOL: Threat of Loss

The solution to FOL is LOF.

Honor Christ in Speech too

Q: My girlfriend keeps getting after me because I use words like "God" and "Jesus" in my ordinary speech. I don't mean anything by it or think of them as cusswords, and anyway, everyone uses them (even on TV), but she says I ought to be more respectful. Would you agree with her?—J.McD.

A: I know using the divine name in ordinary speech has become very common today but, yes, I would agree with your girlfriend. The Bible is very clear: "You shall not misuse the name of the Lord your God, for the Lord will not hold anyone guiltless who misuses his name" (Exodus 20:7).

Why is this? In your letter, you say that you "don't mean anything by it," but if you stop to think about it, this is exactly what is wrong with it. In other words, your speech shows that you have a very casual attitude toward God and toward Jesus Christ, and that they mean very little to you. Your girlfriend senses this, and I hope you'll be grateful for her spiritual sensitivity.

But should we ignore God as if he is unworthy of our respect? Or should we treat Jesus Christ as if his death on the cross for us is unimportant? No, of course not. After all, God maybe unimportant to you but you aren't unimportant to him. God made you, and he not only made you, but he loves you and sent his son into the world to give his life for you. You are that important to him. My prayer is that you will face your need of God and open your heart and life to Jesus Christ. Don't be swayed by the crowd, but have the courage to honor Christ in everything—including your speech.

Billy Graham

Tribune Media Services

www.ingramcontent.com/pod-product-compliance
Lightning Source LLC
Chambersburg PA
CBHW070449050426
42451CB00015B/3410